San Francisco Giants 2019

A Baseball Companion

Edited by Patrick Dubuque, Aaron Gleeman and Bret Sayre

Baseball Prospectus

Craig Brown and Dave Pease, Consultant Editors
Rob McQuown and Harry Pavlidis, Statistics Editors

Copyright © 2019 by DIY Baseball, LLC.
All rights reserved

This book or any part thereof may not be reproduced or transmitted in any form or by any means, electronic or mechanical, including photocopying, recording, or by any information storage and retrieval system, without permission in writing from the publisher.

Limit of Liability/Disclaimer of Warranty: While the publisher and the author have used their best efforts in preparing this book, they make no representations or warranties with respect to the accuracy or completeness of the contents of this book and specifically disclaim any implied warranties of merchantability or fitness for a particular purpose. No warranty may be created or extended by sales representatives or written sales materials. The advice and strategies contained herein may not be suitable for your situation. You should consult with a professional where appropriate. Neither the publisher nor the author shall be liable for any loss of profit or any other commercial damages, including but not limited to special, incidental, consequential, or other damages.

Library of Congress Cataloging-in-Publication Data:
paperback
ISBN-13: 978-1-949332-54-4

Project Credits
Cover Design: Kathleen Dyson
Interior Design and Production: Jeff Pease, Dave Pease
Layout: Jeff Pease, Dave Pease

Baseball icon courtesy of Uberux, from https://www.shareicon.net/author/uberux

Ballpark diagram courtesy of Lou Spirito/THIRTY81 Project, https://thirty81project.com/

Manufactured in the United States of America
10 9 8 7 6 5 4 3 2 1

Table of Contents

Foreword v
    Rob Mains

Statistical Introduction vii

Part 1: Team Analysis

Table for Two: Previewing the 2019 San Francisco Giants 3
    Rich MacLeod and Bret Sayre

Performance Graphs 7

2018 Team Performance 8

2019 Team Projections 9

Team Personnel 10

Oracle Park Stats 11

Giants Team Analysis 13

Part 2: Player Analysis

Giants Player Analysis 20

Giants Prospects 107

Part 3: Featured Articles

The Hole in The Shift is Fixing Itself 119
    Russell Carleton

The State of the Quality Start 123
    Rob Mains

Heads-Up Hacking—The First Pitch 129
    Matthew Trueblood

A Hymn for the Index Stat 135
    Patrick Dubuque

Index of Names 139

Foreword

Rob Mains

Welcome to this companion of the 2019 San Francisco Giants. We at Baseball Prospectus are excited to provide this analysis of the Giants.

Our website, Baseball Prospectus, is a leader in delivering high-quality commentary and data to baseball fans everywhere. To some, those words—commentary and data—appear mutually exclusive. There are people out there who believe that traditional analysis and advanced analytics must run on different paths. But the simplistic narrative of stats vs. traditionalists just isn't true. Every team's analytics department interacts with scouting, development, and major league operations with a common goal: Delivering a championship. New technologies, like radar tracking of pitch speeds and movement, enable talent evaluators to focus on qualitative aspects of pitching like mechanics and pitch sequencing. In-game strategies like infield shifts, based on batters' hit tendencies, help turn balls in play into outs. Hitters use information to adjust their swings to maximize run production.

All these numbers can seem, at best, intimidating, and at worst, counterproductive to the casual fan. Even as technology and analysis have embedded themselves deeply into the way teams run, it can often feel like statistics create a displacement between the viewer and the sport, breaking them out of the action. And yet every fan incorporates the numbers to some degree; stats like batting average and earned run average, so fundamental to how we talk about performance, are actually complicated formulas. They don't bother people because those formulas have become second nature, as easy to translate as the action on the field.

Along the way, new statistics have entered baseball's lexicon. You'll see some of them, like on-base percentage (which measures a batter's ability to get on base via walk, hit batter, or hit), OPS (on-base plus slugging), and average exit velocity (the speed of balls off a hitter's bat) on broadcasts. Others, like DRC+, might well be new to you. Some of them have been well-defined to the public, others haven't. That lack of context has created ambiguity. Fans know that a ball hit 100 mph is scorched, but does that mean extra bases? (Not if it's hit on the ground or high in the air it doesn't.)

For those who are amenable to them, the new statistics can increase the enjoyment and understanding of the game. They can help fans identify when a pitcher is tiring, when a stolen base or a bunt attempt makes sense (and, more often, when it doesn't), or how a team's lineup might be constructed. Websites like Baseball Prospectus add to that understanding by weaving metrics into the narrative of the game. That's the goal of this publication: to take some of the newer, more complicated statistics and make them as intuitive as the ones on the back of old baseball cards.

But you don't need to love analytics to love baseball. The fans at BP who worked together to write this guide are captivated first and foremost by the game itself. We're drawn to Aaron Judge's power, Francisco Lindor's glove, Billy Hamilton's speed and Patrick Corbin's slider and don't need numbers to tell us why they're so mesmerizing. The underlying statistics provide depth to the game that we all love.

We hope you'll find that this guide helps you better understand the Giants. Our analysts have studied the team's major league personnel and its minor league affiliates to identify their strengths and weaknesses, both the obvious ones and those that only a careful dissection of players' performances—yes, including the data—can reveal. You don't need us to tell you who was good and who wasn't in 2018, but our models and writers can help you project how each player is going to perform this year and beyond, and appreciate the greatness of each new game as it unfolds. As in the sport itself, the human and analytic components combine to generate a deeper overall understanding.

Think back to the first time you saw a baseball game on a high-definition TV. You'd grown familiar with how the game looked and felt on a picture tube. But new TV allowed you to see details that you'd never seen before. That's how advanced statistics work. The game itself is why you're here and why you're buying this. (And, for that matter, why we wrote it.) The statistical measures provide the sharper focus, the detail, the depth of knowledge that you didn't have before, generating an overall superior picture. Enjoy the view.

—Rob Mains is an author of Baseball Prospectus.

Statistical Introduction

Sports are, fundamentally, a blend of athletic endeavor and storytelling. Baseball, like any other sport, tells its stories in so many ways: in the arc of a game from the stands or a season from the box scores, in photos, or even in numbers. At Baseball Prospectus, we understand that statistics don't replace observation or any of baseball's stories, but complement everything else that makes the game so much fun.

What stats help us with is with patterns and precision, variance and value. This book can help you learn things you may not see from watching a game or hundred, whether it's the path of a career over time or the breadth of the entire MLB. We'd also never ask you to choose between our numbers and the experience of viewing a game from the cheap seats or the comfort of your home; our publication combines running the numbers with observations and wisdom from some of the brightest minds we can find. But if you *do* want to learn more about the numbers beyond what's on the backs of player jerseys, let us help explain.

Offense

At the end of this past year, we've revised our methodology for determining batting value. Long-time readers of Baseball Prospectus will notice that we've retired True Average in favor of a new metric: Deserved Runs Created Plus (DRC+). Developed by Jonathan Judge and our stats team, this statistic measures everything a player does at the plate–reaching base, hitting for power, making outs, and moving runners over–and puts it on a scale where 100 equals league-average performance. A DRC+ of 150 is terrific, a DRC+ of 100 is average, and a DRC+ of 75 means you better be an excellent defender.

DRC+ also does a better job than any of our previous metrics in taking contextual factors into account. The model adjusts for how the park affects performance, but also for things like the talent of the opposing pitcher, value of different types of batted-ball events, league, temperature, and other factors. It's able to describe a player's expected offensive contribution than any other statistic we've found over the years, and also does a better job of predicting future performance as well.

The other aspect of run-scoring is baserunning, which we quantify using Baserunning Runs. BRR not only records the value of stolen bases (or getting caught in the act), but also accounts for a runner's ability to go first to third on a single or advance on a fly ball.

Defense

Where offensive value is *relatively* easy to identify and understand, defensive value is ... not. Over the past dozen years, the sabermetric community has focused mostly on stats based on zone data: a real-live human person records the type of batted ball and estimated landing location, and models are created that give expected outs. From there, you can compare fielders' actual outs to those expected ones. Simple, right?

Unfortunately, zone data has two major issues. First, zone data is recorded by commercial data providers who keep the raw data private unless you pay for it. (All the statistics we build in this book and on our website use public data as inputs.) That hurts our ability to test assumptions or duplicate results. Second, over the years it has become apparent that there's quite a bit of "noise" in zone-based fielding analysis. Sometimes the conclusions drawn from zone data don't hold up to scrutiny, and sometimes the different data provided by different providers don't look anything alike, giving wildly different results. Sometimes the hard-working professional stringers or scorers might unknowingly inflict unconscious bias into the mix: for example good fielders will often be credited with more expected outs despite the data, and ballparks with high press boxes tend to score more line drives than ones with a lower press box.

Enter our Fielding Runs Above Average (FRAA). For most positions, FRAA is built from play-by-play data, which allows us to avoid the subjectivity found in many other fielding metrics. The idea is this: count how many fielding plays are made by a given player and compare that to expected plays for an average fielder at their position (based on pitcher ground-ball tendencies and batter handedness). Then we adjust for park and base-out situations.

When it comes to catchers, our methodology is a little different thanks to the laundry list of responsibilities they're tasked with beyond just, well, catching and throwing the ball. By now you've probably heard about "framing" or the art of making umpires more likely to call balls outside the strike zone for strikes. To put this into one tidy number, we incorporate pitch tracking data (for the years it exists) and adjust for important factors like pitcher, umpire, batter, and home-field advantage using a mixed-model approach. This grants us a number for how many strikes the catcher is personally adding to (or subtracting from) his pitchers' performance ... which we then convert to runs added or lost using linear weights.

Framing is one of the biggest parts of determining catcher value, but we also take into account blocking balls from going past, whether a scorer deems it a passed ball or a wild pitch. We use a similar approach–one that really benefits from the pitch tracking data that tells us what ends up in the dirt and what doesn't. We also include a catcher's ability to prevent stolen bases and how well they field balls in play, and *finally* we come up with our FRAA for catchers.

Pitching

Both pitching and fielding make up the half of baseball that isn't run scoring: run prevention. Separating pitching from fielding is a tough task, and most recent pitching analysis has branched off from Voros McCracken's famous (and controversial) statement, "There is little if any difference among major-league pitchers in their ability to prevent hits on balls hit in the field of play." The research of the analytic community has validated this to some extent, and there are a host of "defense-independent" pitching measures that have been developed to try and extricate the effect of the defense behind a hurler from the pitcher's work.

Our solution to this quandry is Deserved Run Average (DRA), our core pitching metric. DRA looks like earned run average (ERA), the tried-and-true pitching stat you've seen on every baseball broadcast or box score from the past century, but it's very different. To start, DRA takes an event-by-event look at what the pitchers does, and adjusts the value of that event based on different environmental factors like park, batter, catcher, umpire, base-out situation, run differential, inning, defense, home field advantage, pitcher role, and temperature. That mixed model gives us a pitcher's expected contribution, similar to what we do for our DRC+ model for hitters and FRAA model for catchers. (Oh, and we also consider the pitcher's effect on basestealing and on balls getting past the catcher.)

It's important to note that DRA is set to the scale of runs allowed per nine innings (RA9) instead of ERA, which makes DRA's scale slightly higher than ERA's. The reason for this is because ERA tends to overrate three types of pitchers:

1. Pitchers who play in parks where scorers hand out more errors. Official scorers differ significantly in the frequency at which they assign errors to fielders.
2. Ground-ball pitchers, because a substantial proportion of errors occur on grounders.
3. Pitchers who aren't very good. Better pitchers often allow fewer unearned runs than bad pitchers, because good pitchers tend to find ways to get out of jams.

Since the last time you picked up an edition of this book, we've also made a few minor changes to DRA to make it better. Recent research into "tunneling"–the act of throwing consecutive pitches that appear similar from a batter's point of view until after the swing decision point–data has given us a new contextual factor to account for in DRA: plate distance. This refers to the distance between successive pitches as they approach the plate, and while it has a smaller effect than factors like velocity or whiff rate, it still can help explain pitcher strikeout rate in our model.

New Pitching Metrics for 2019

We're including a few "new" pitching metrics for 2019's suite of Baseball Prospectus publications, but you may be familiar with them if you've spent time scouring the internet for stats.

Fastball Percentage

Our fastball percentage (FB%) statistic measures how frequently a pitcher throws a pitch classified as a "fastball," measured as a percentage of overall pitches thrown. We qualify three types of fastballs:

1. The traditional four-seam fastball;
2. The two-seam fastball or sinker;
3. "Hard cutters," which are pitches that have the movement profile of a cut fastball and are used as the pitcher's primary offering or in place of a more traditional fastball.

For example, a pitcher with a FB% of 67 throws any combination of these three pitches about two-thirds of the time.

Whiff Rate

Everybody loves a swing and a miss, and whiff rate (WHF) measures how frequently pitchers induce a swinging strike. To calculate WHF, we add up all the pitches thrown that ended with a swinging strike, then divide that number by a pitcher's total pitches thrown. Most often, high whiff rates correlate with high strikeout rates (and overall effective pitcher performance).

Called Strike Probability

Called Strike Probability (CSP) is a number that represents the likelihood that all of a pitcher's pitches will be called a strike while controlling for location, pitcher and batter handedness, umpire and count. Here's how it works: on each pitch, our model determines how many times (out of 100) that a similar pitch was called for a strike given those factors mentioned above, and when normalized for each batter's strike zone. Then we average the CSP for all pitches thrown by a pitcher in a season, and that gives us the yearly CSP percentage you see in the stats boxes.

As you might imagine, pitchers with a higher CSP are more likely to work in the zone, where pitchers with a lower CSP are likely locating their pitches outside the normal strike zone, for better or for worse.

Projections

Many of you aren't turning to this book just for a look at what a player has done, but for a look at what a player is going to do: the PECOTA projections. PECOTA, initially developed by Nate Silver (who has moved on to greater fame as a political analyst), consists of three parts:

1. Major-league equivalencies, which use minor-league statistics to project how a player will perform in the major leagues;
2. Baseline forecasts, which use weighted averages and regression to the mean to estimate a player's current true talent level; and
3. Aging curves, which uses the career paths of comparable players to estimate how a player's statistics are likely to change over time.

With all those important things covered, let's take a look at what's in the book this year.

Team Prospectus

You bought this book to learn more about your favorite (or maybe least-favorite, who are we to judge?) team, so let's talk about them. After a thoughtful preview of the 2019 season, you'll be presented with our Team Prospectus. This outlines many of the key statistics for each team's 2018 season, as well as a very inviting stadium diagram.

First you'll find the Performance Graphs page. The first is the 2018 Hit List Ranking. This shows our Hit List Rank for the team on each day of the 2018 season and is intended to give you a picture of the ups and downs of the team's season, including their highest and lowest ranks of the year. Hit List Rank measures overall team performance and drives the Hit List Power Rankings at the baseballprospectus.com website.

The second graph is Committed Payroll and helps you see how the team's payroll has compared to the MLB and divisional average payrolls over time. Payroll figures are currents as of January 1, 2019; with so many free agents still unsigned as of this writing, the final 2018 figure will likely be significantly different for many teams. (In the meantime, you can always find the most current data at Baseball Prospectus' Cot's Baseball Contracts page.)

San Francisco Giants 2019

The third graph is Farm System Ranking and displays how the Baseball Prospectus prospect team has ranked the organization's farm system since 2007. It also indicates the highest and lowest ranks that the farm system achieved over that time.

We start the Team Performance page with the squad's unadjusted and third-order 2018 win-loss records, presented in divisional context. We then list the three highest performing hitters and pitchers by WARP for 2018. Beneath that are a host of other team statistics. **Pythag** presents an adjusted 2018 winning percentage, calculated by taking runs scored per game (**RS/G**) and runs allowed per game (**RA/G**) for the team, and running them through a version of Bill James' Pythagorean formula that was refined and improved by David Smyth and Brandon Heipp. (The formula is called "Pythagenpat," which is equally fun to type and to say.)

Next up is **DRC+**, described earlier, to indicate the overall hitting ability of the team either above or below league-average. Run prevention on the pitching side is covered by **DRA** (also mentioned earlier) and another metric: Fielding Independent Pitching (**FIP**), which calculates another ERA-like statistic based on strikeouts, walks, and home runs recorded. Defensive Efficiency Rating (**DER**) tells us the percentage of balls in play turned into outs for the team, and is a quick fielding shorthand that rounds out run prevention.

After that, we have several measures related to roster composition, as opposed to on-field performance. **B-Age** and **P-Age** tell us the average age of a team's batters and pitchers, respectively. **Salary** is the combined team payroll for all on-field players, and Doug Pappas' Marginal Dollars per Marginal Win (**M$/MW**) tells us how much money a team spent to earn production above replacement level.

Ending this batch of statistics is the number of disabled list days a team had over the season (**DL Days**) and the amount of salary paid to players on the disabled list (**$ on DL**); this final number is expressed as a percentage of total payroll.

Next to each of these stats, we've listed each team's MLB rank in that category from 1st to 30th. In this, 1st always indicates a positive outcome and 30th a negative outcome, except in the case of salary–1st is highest.

The Team Projections page is intended to convey the team's operational capacity entering the 2019 season. We start with the team's PECOTA projected record for 2019, again in divisional context. The **+/-** column indicates how many more or less wins the team is projected to get than they got in 2018. We then list the three highest projected hitters and pitchers by WARP for 2018. A brief farm system summary follows, with the team's top prospect and number of BP Top 101 Prospects. Finally, we list the key new players and departed players, along with their 2019 projected WARP.

www.baseballprospectus.com

Alex Bregman 3B
Born: 03/30/94 Age: 25 Bats: R Throws: R
Height: 6'0" Weight: 180 Origin: Round 1, 2015 Draft (#2 overall)

YEAR	TEAM	LVL	AGE	PA	R	2B	3B	HR	RBI	BB	K	SB	CS	AVG/OBP/SLG
2016	CCH	AA	22	285	54	16	2	14	46	42	26	5	3	.297/.415/.559
2016	FRE	AAA	22	83	17	6	0	6	15	5	12	2	1	.333/.373/.641
2016	HOU	MLB	22	217	31	13	3	8	34	15	52	2	0	.264/.313/.478
2017	HOU	MLB	23	626	88	39	5	19	71	55	97	17	5	.284/.352/.475
2018	HOU	MLB	24	705	105	51	1	31	103	96	85	10	4	.286/.394/.532
2019	HOU	MLB	25	675	96	38	3	23	78	73	107	12	4	.272/.359/.463

Breakout: 6%   Improve: 52%   Collapse: 5%   Attrition: 2%   MLB: 100%
Comparables: Anthony Rendon, David Wright, Pablo Sandoval

YEAR	TEAM	LVL	AGE	PA	DRC+	VORP	BABIP	BRR	FRAA	WARP
2016	CCH	AA	22	285	172	38.9	.286	1.6	SS(51): -3.4, 3B(11): 1.4	2.7
2016	FRE	AAA	22	83	161	10.0	.333	-1.2	SS(14): 2.1, LF(3): -0.1	0.8
2016	HOU	MLB	22	217	107	9.6	.317	0.5	3B(40): 0.9, SS(6): -0.1	1.1
2017	HOU	MLB	23	626	114	34.7	.311	-1.5	3B(132): 8.7, SS(30): -2.9	3.9
2018	HOU	MLB	24	705	150	72.6	.289	-1.6	3B(136): 5.4, SS(28): -0.4	7.4
2019	HOU	MLB	25	675	125	37.3	.295	0.0	3B 7, SS 0	4.6

After the projections page, we share a few items about the team's home ballpark. There's the aforementioned diagram of the park's dimensions (including distances to the outfield wall), a few important biographical facts about the stadium, a graphic showing the height of the wall from the left-field pole to the right-field pole, and a table showing three-year park factors for the stadium. The park factors are displayed as indexes where 100 is average, 110 means that the park inflates the statistic in question by 10 percent, and 90 means that the park deflates the statistic in question by 10 percent.

Following the ballpark page, we have a **Personnel** section that lists many of the important decision-makers and upper-level field and operations staff members for the franchise, as well as any former Baseball Prospectus staff members who are currently part of the organization.

Position Players

After all that information and a thoughtful bylined essay covering each team, we present our player comments. Each player is listed with the major-league team who employed him as of early January 2019. If a player changed teams after that point via free agency, trade, or any other method, you'll be able to find them in the book for their previous squad.

First, we cover biographical information (age is as of June 30, 2019) before moving onto the stats themselves. Our statistic columns include standard identifying information like **YEAR**, **TEAM**, **LVL** (level of affiliated play) and **AGE** before getting into the numbers. Next, we provide raw, unstranslated numbers like you might find on the back of your dad's baseball cards: **PA** (plate appearances), **R** (runs), **2B** (doubles), **3B** (triples), **HR** (home runs), **RBI** (runs batted in), **BB** (walks), **K** (strikeouts), **SB** (stolen bases) and **CS** (caught stealing). Then we have unadjusted "slash" statistics: **AVG** (batting average), **OBP** (on-base percentage) and **SLG** (slugging percentage).

Just below the stats box is **PECOTA** data, which is discussed further in a following section. After that, it's on to a pithy and always-informative comment written by a member of the Baseball Prospectus staff, before we cover more stats.

The second text box repeats YEAR, TEAM, LVL, AGE, and PA, then moves on to **DRC+** (Deserved Runs Created Plus), which we described earlier as total offensive expected contribution compared to the league average. Next, one of our oldest active metrics, **VORP** (Value Over Replacement Player), considers offensive production, position and plate appearances. In essence, it is the number of runs contributed beyond what a replacement-level player at the same position would contribute if given the same percentage of team plate appearances. VORP does not consider the quality of a player's defense.

BABIP (batting average on balls in play) tells us how often a ball in play fell for a hit, and can help us identify whether a batter may have been lucky or not … but note that high BABIPs also tend to follow the great hitters of our time, as well as speedy singles hitters who put the ball on the ground.

The next item is **BRR** (Baserunning Runs), which covers all of a player's baserunning accomplishments which includes (but isn't limited to) swiped bags and failed attempts. Next is **FRAA** (Fielding Runs Above Average), which also includes the number of games previously played at each position noted in parentheses. Multi-position players have only their two most frequent positions listed here, but their total FRAA number reflects all positions played.

Our last column here is **WARP** (Wins Above Replacement Player). WARP estimates the total value of a player, which means for hitters it takes into account hitting runs above average (calculated using the DRC+ model), BRR and FRAA. Then, it makes an adjustment for positions played and gives the player a credit for plate appearances based upon the difference between "replacement level"¬–which is derived from the quality of players added to a team's roster after the start of the season¬–and the league average.

Catchers

Catchers are a special breed, and thus they have earned their own separate box which displays some of the defensive metrics that we've built just for them. As an example, let's check out J.T. Realmuto.

YEAR	TEAM	P. COUNT	FRM RUNS	BLK RUNS	THRW RUNS	TOT RUNS
2016	MIA	18935	-8.5	1.8	2.1	-5.6
2017	MIA	18959	5.3	1.7	1.0	9.1
2018	MIA	16399	-0.4	0.9	0.1	0.4
2019	PHI	18448	-1.4	1.5	0.7	0.8

The **YEAR** and **TEAM** columns match what you'd find in the other stat box. **P. COUNT** indicates the number of pitches thrown while the catcher was behind the plate, including swinging strikes, fouls, and balls in play. **FRM RUNS** is the total run value the catcher provided (or cost) his team by influencing the umpire to call strikes where other catchers did not. **BLK RUNS** expresses the total run value above or below average for the catcher's ability to prevent wild pitches and passed balls. **THRW RUNS** is calculated using a similar model as the previous two statistics, and it measures a catcher's ability to throw out basestealers but also to dissuade them from testing his arm in the first place. It takes into account factors like the pitcher (including his delivery and pickoff move) and baserunner (who could be as fast as Billy Hamilton or as slow as Yonder Alonso). **TOT RUNS** is the sum of all of the previous three statistics.

Pitchers

Let's give our pitchers a turn, using 2018 NL Cy Young winner Jacob deGrom as our example. Take a look at his first stat block: the first line and the **YEAR**, **TEAM**, **LVL** and **AGE** columns are the same as in the position player example earlier.

Here too, we have a series of columns that display raw, unadjusted statistics compiled by the pitcher over the course of a season: **W** (wins), **L** (losses), **SV** (saves), **G** (games pitched), **GS** (games started), **IP** (innings pitched), **H** (hits allowed) and **HR** (home runs allowed). Next we have two statistics that are rates: **BB/9** (walks per nine innings) and **K/9** (strikeouts per nine innings), before returning to the unadjusted **K** (strikeouts).

Next up is **GB%** (ground ball percentage), which is the percentage of all batted balls that were hit in the ground, including both outs and hits. Remember, this is based on observational data and subject to human error, so please approach this with a healthy dose of skepticism.

BABIP (batting average on balls in play) is calculated using the same methodology as it is for position players, but it often tells us more about a pitcher than it does a hitter. With pitchers, a high BABIP is often due to poor defense or bad luck, and can often be an indicator of potential rebound, and a low BABIP may be cause to expect performance regression. (A typical league-average BABIP is close to .290-.300.)

After a witty 150ish words on the player like only Baseball Prospectus's staff can provide, it's on to that second stat block, which repeats the YEAR, TEAM, LVL, and AGE columns. The metrics **WHIP** (walks plus hits per inning pitched) and **ERA**

San Francisco Giants 2019

(earned run average) are old standbys: WHIP measures walks and hits allowed on a per-inning basis, while ERA measures earned runs on a nine-inning basis. Neither of these stats are translated or adjusted.

DRA (Deserved Run Average) was described at length earlier, and measures how many runs the pitcher "deserved" to allow per nine innings. Please note that since we lack all the data points that would make for a "real" DRA for minor-league events, the DRA displayed for minor league partial-seasons is based off of different data. (That data is a modified version of our cFIP metric, which you can find more information about on our website.)

Jacob deGrom   RHP

Born: 06/19/88   Age: 31   Bats: L   Throws: R
Height: 6'4"   Weight: 180   Origin: Round 9, 2010 Draft (#272 overall)

YEAR	TEAM	LVL	AGE	W	L	SV	G	GS	IP	H	HR	BB/9	K/9	K	GB%	BABIP
2016	NYN	MLB	28	7	8	0	24	24	148	142	15	2.2	8.7	143	47%	.312
2017	NYN	MLB	29	15	10	0	31	31	201[1]	180	28	2.6	10.7	239	48%	.305
2018	NYN	MLB	30	10	9	0	32	32	217	152	10	1.9	11.2	269	48%	.281
2019	NYN	MLB	31	13	9	0	31	31	186	145	18	2.3	10.7	221	46%	.286

Breakout: 8%   Improve: 29%   Collapse: 28%   Attrition: 6%   MLB: 85%
Comparables: Erik Bedard, A.J. Burnett, CC Sabathia

YEAR	TEAM	LVL	AGE	WHIP	ERA	DRA	WARP	MPH	FB%	WHF	CSP
2016	NYN	MLB	28	1.20	3.04	3.30	3.5	96.3	59.6	12.1	47.2
2017	NYN	MLB	29	1.19	3.53	3.02	5.7	97.2	55.5	14.5	49.5
2018	NYN	MLB	30	0.91	1.70	2.09	8.0	98.2	52.1	16.3	48.4
2019	NYN	MLB	31	1.02	2.91	3.23	3.9	96.6	54.5	14.8	48.2

Just like with hitters, **WARP** (Wins Above Replacement Player) is a total value metric that puts pitchers of all stripes on the same scale as position players. We use DRA as the primary input for our calculation of WARP. You might notice that relief pitchers (due to their limited innings) may have a lower WARP than you were expecting or than you might see in other WARP-like metrics. WARP does not take leverage into account, just the actions a pitcher performs and the expected value of those actions ... which ends up judging high-leverage relief pitchers differently than you might imagine given their prestige and market value.

MPH gives you the pitcher's 95th percentile velocity for the noted season, in order to give you an idea of what the *peak* fastball velocity a pitcher possesses. Since this comes from our pitch tracking data, it is not publicly available for minor-league pitchers.

Finally, we display the three new pitching metrics we described earlier. **FB%** (fastball percentage) gives you the percentage of fastballs thrown out of all pitches. **WhiffRt** (whiff rate) tells you the percentage of swinging strikes induced out of all pitches. **CS Prob** (called strike probability) expresses the likelihood of all pitches thrown to result in a called strike, after controlling for factors like handedness, umpire, pitch type, count, and location.

PECOTA

All players have PECOTA projections for 2019, as well as a set of other numbers that describe the performance of comparable players according to PECOTA. All projections for 2019 are for the player at the date we went to press in early January and are projected into the league and park context as indicated by the team abbreviation. All PECOTA projected statistics represent a player's projected major-league performance.

The numbers beneath the player's stats–Breakout, Improve, Collapse, Attrition–are part and parcel of the PECOTA projections. They estimate the likelihood of changes in performance relative to the player's previously-established level of production, based on the performance of comparable players:

Breakout Rate is the percent change that a player's production will improve by at least 20 percent relative to the weighted average of his performance over his most recent seasons.

Improve Rate is the percent chance that a player's production will improve at all relative to his baseline performance. A player who is expected to perform just the same as he has in the recent past will have an Improve Rate of 50 percent.

Collapse Rate is the percent chance that a position player's production will decline by at least 25 percent relative to his baseline performance.

Attrition Rate operates on playing time rather than performance. Specifically, it measures the likelihood that a player's playing time will decrease by at least 50 percent relative to his established level.

Breakout Rate and Collapse Rate can sometimes be counterintuitive for players who have already experienced a radical change in performance level. It's also worth noting that the projected decline in a player's rate performances might not be indicative of an expected decline in underlying ability or skill, but could just be an anticipated correction following a breakout season.

MLB% is the percentage of similar players who played in the major leagues in their relevant season.

The final pieces of information are the player's three highest-scoring comparable players as determined by PECOTA. All comparables represent a snapshot of how the listed player was performing at the same age as the current player, so if a 23-year-old pitcher is compared to Bartolo Colon, he's actually being compared to a 23-year-old Colon, not the version that pitched for the Rangers in 2018, nor to Colon's career as a whole.

San Francisco Giants 2019

A few points about pitcher projections. First, we aren't yet projecting peak velocity, so that column will be blank in the PECOTA lines. Second, projecting DRA is trickier than evaluating past performance, because it is unclear how deserving each pitcher will be of his anticipated outcomes. However, we know that another DRA-related statistic–contextual FIP or cFIP–estimates future run scoring very well. So for PECOTA, the projected DRA figures you see are based on the past cFIPs generated by the pitcher and comparable players over time, along with the other factors described above.

Lineouts

In each chapter's Lineouts section, you'll find abbreviated text comments, as well as most of same information you'd find in our full player comments. We limit the stats boxes in this section to only including the 2018 information for each player.

Exclusive Player Visualizations

In our constant battle to provide you with new and interesting baseball content you can't find anywhere else, we've added a trio of data visualizations to each hitter's entry in these books and a pair of visualizations for each pitcher.

For hitters, you'll find three new infographics. The first is each player's **Batted Ball Distribution**, which displays the five major sections of the field: LF (left), LCF (left center), CF (center), RCF (right center), and RF (right). The percentage indicated tells us what percentage of batted balls from that hitter fell within that part of the field during the 2018 season. We've also included the hitter's slugging percentage on balls in play (also called **SLGCON**) for that part of the field.

You'll also see two heatmaps: **Strike Zone vs LHP** and **Strike Zone vs RHP**. These heat maps represent a view of the strike zone from behind the catcher. Areas where there is a darker coloration represent the places where a higher percentage of pitches resulted in hits. In other words, the heatmap represents a hitter's "sweet spots" for getting hits against either left-handed or right-handed pitchers, depending on the image.

Pitchers get two images that help explain what their pitches look like from a hitter's perspective: **Pitch Shape vs LHH** and **Pitch Shape vs RHH**. These images show you the shape and the "tunneling" effect of each pitcher's offerings from the batter's perspective. For each type of pitch that a pitcher throws (represented by an indicator shape), there's a set of dots indicating the flight path, where each dot represents a 0.01-second interval. This maps the average trajectory and speed of an offering, ending where the ball crosses the plate. The solid black box represents the regular strike zone, while the gray contour lines indicate the range of locations that a pitcher typically works in.

Below the image, we provide a bit more detailed information about each pitcher's average offering in the **Pitch Types** box. Here, we also list each of the pitcher's major offerings under the **Type** column.

- **Fastballs** (which usually refers to the four-seam variation)
- **Sinkers** and/or two-seam fastballs
- **Cutters** (which could include "hard" cutters like cut fastballs and "soft" cutters that resemble hard sliders)
- **Changeups** (not including most splitters)
- **Splitters** (split-fingered pitches, forkballs, and some split-changes)
- **Sliders** and/or slurves
- **Curveballs** (including spike-curveballs and knuckle-curveballs, as well as some slurvy curves)
- **Slow curveballs** and/or eephus pitches
- **Knuckleballs**
- **Screwballs**

The **Freq** column indicates the percentage of overall pitches that fall into each of those type categories; if a pitcher has a 16.55% score for changeups, then that's the percent of all pitches that he throws as changeups. **Velo** is exactly what you think it is: the average miles per hour for each pitch type. **H Mov** is the number of inches of horizontal movement on the average pitch of that type, while **V Mov** is the number of inches of vertical movement on the average pitch of that type. (At Baseball Prospectus, we measure this over the long flight of the ball and include gravity into the V Mov number in order to give you the most realistic representation of what the pitch *actually* does.)

If you're wondering about the second number in brackets, that's the index for that velocity or movement compared to the league average. Like DRC+, a score of 100 means that the speed or movement is about the same as league average, while a higher score means that there's higher velocity or movement than the league average. Numbers below 100 indicate less velocity or movement than the league average.

Part 1: Team Analysis

Table for Two: Previewing the 2019 San Francisco Giants

Rich MacLeod and Bret Sayre

RICH MACLEOD: Dread it. Run from it. Destiny arrives all the same. And now it's here…the 2019 San Francisco Giants season.

/loud crashing noise

BRET SAYRE: I mean, it would be awfully lazy for us to just declare it an odd year and write off the Giants, but this particular version of the team has far more reasons to quell optimism than just the calendar. In some ways, it's a very Giants team because it would be a strong contender for the 2014 World Series. (Of course, they already won it once so trying for it again seems pointless, but we've all played video games over and over at differing levels to try and beat ourselves.) It's also a very Giants team because many of its roster spots are filled with homegrown players you've never heard of and probably will never remember. Right now they're lined up to start Mac Williamson, Steven Duggar and Austin Slater on the grass (Who needs Bryce Harper indeed?) and if you told me they were starting Zack Morris, Samuel Powers and A.C. Slater, I wouldn't bat an eye.

Which brings us to our first question: is it possible for someone to actually fall short of expectations on this team and collapse? And if so, who is it?

RICH: Man, that's a tough one. Considering that projections for the Giants' young crop of players (a real who's who of "who?") are pretty conservative, I'd look more towards the guys who the majority of fans actually know about. I think Madison Bumgarner and Evan Longoria are certainly candidates to underperform PECOTA's expectations, but I'm going to take it one step further.

This may be blasphemous to say in San Francisco, but are we really sure that Buster Posey is capable of a 120 DRC+ and 4.8 WARP? He's been undoubtedly one of the game's best catchers over the last decade, but there's a lot of wear-and-tear after 10 years of catching, three long postseason runs and a few season-ending surgeries. In two of the last three seasons, Posey has been slightly above league average according to DRC+, and while he did post a mark of 129 in 2017, I'm not so sure he's going to be that player anymore. Posey will be 32 years old on Opening Day and underwent right hip surgery just six months ago. So, while I don't foresee a "collapse" by any means, I do think it's pretty fair to wonder if we see a steadying decline from here on out.

BRET: Seems like part of the Giants strategy is to build around players who are aging and accumulating injuries these days, and they're hitting all their marks. But honestly, I look at their projections and they all feel very reachable. Sure, we've seen the best of Madison Bumgarner, but if he makes 27 starts and doesn't surpass the 1.4 WARP he's projected for, I'll be shocked. I'd make the exact same argument for Brandon Crawford on the offensive side. I guess the only number I look at a little sideways is the projected playing time for Brandon Belt. The numbers seem realistic—114 DRC+ with 15 homers—but he's topped out at 456 plate appearances the last two years and expecting 500-plus with his injury history (especially given the concussions) is a little rosier than I'd feel comfortable with.

Of course, this is all to say that the Giants are torn between two worlds right now. They have too much talent on their major-league team to be tanking and they have too little in the way of quality prospects to be successfully rebuilding…yet. What shape do we think this team will take during the course of 2019? Will they get enough surprising bounce backs to give them a glimmer of hope, or will the season play out as expected and Bumgarner, the impending free agent, becomes one of the biggest trade chips available around midseason?

RICH: Okay, so I'm going to make a comparison that's not totally fair but has some merit to it. This kind of reminds me a lot of the 2017 Kansas City Royals club. After a couple big postseason runs, and a lot of trades in the meantime to make those possible, this is now an older roster made up of players whose hay days are all behind them along with a minor league system that isn't on the brink of producing key major league players.

The Royals hung on a little too long, as they half-heartedly "went for it" in 2016 and 2017 by choosing to add, not subtract, at the trade deadlines. They knew players like Eric Hosmer and Lorenzo Cain were going to be leaving and opted to hold onto them for a run that never materialized. Now, I do think the Giants are in somewhat better shape in their farm system and are far more capable of spending in free agency down the line when they're ready to contend again, but there are quite a few similarities here.

Even if they manage to get off to a decent start, which is probably their ceiling in 2019, I think it would be wise for them to avoid the mistakes of teams past and sell off whatever veteran pieces that aren't going to be a part of their future. Guys like Madison Bumgarner, Evan Longoria, Brandon Crawford and probably even Brandon Belt should all be deemed as available for the right price. As we've learned from the '17 Royals and even the '12 Phillies, holding on for too long makes your eventual rebuild that more difficult. And it's hard to see any near-future scenario for the Giants that doesn't involve a rebuilding period.

BRET: I mean, sure, but who's buying these players unless the Giants are heavily subsidizing them? Crawford has three years and nearly $46 million left on his contract and mid-30s shortstops ain't quite the most attractive trade chips to start (even the ones who still provide high-end defense). Belt has nearly $52 million his deal left and it's for the same period of time. But both of them pale in comparison to the $73 million plus left on Longoria's deal that extends through at least 2022.

That basically gives them one shot at this, and like a lot of their last 6-7 years, it all falls on Madison Bumgarner's burly left shoulder. If he comes out this year, reclaims his stuff and pitches like the pre-dirt bike accident version of himself, they could get a strong package for him at the deadline that could help really pad their farm system. After all, it's not just that they don't have many impact prospects, but like the Royals you compared them to earlier, they just don't have the depth in the minors to compete with these other systems—particularly in a division with four deep organizations, including the best farm team in the majors.

Given the situation they find themselves in, how should they have approached this offseason? We know basically the full extent of what they've done at this point, and it hasn't been much. Should they have been more aggressive in grabbing players they could have flipped at the deadline to add more depth to their farm system? Should they have signed a major-league outfielder? Literally, any major-league outfielder?

RICH: While I don't really think there was much the Giants could do this winter to improve their chances at immediate contention, short of signing both Bryce Harper and Manny Machado, I do think they would've been better off signing a handful of free agents that they might be able to flip by the midseason trade deadline rather than bringing in players such as Craig Gentry, Cameron Maybin, Rene Rivera and Derek Holland. Even now, with Spring Training already underway, more attractive players like Dallas Keuchel, Gio Gonzalez, Carlos Gonzalez and Ryan Madson are all available, would fill holes on their roster and should only require one-year commitments.

Judging by what they've done throughout the 2018-19 offseason, the only strategy the Giants have seemed to employ is "we just need to get through this year." And unless they suddenly become far more active and start bringing in flippable assets on discount deals, I'm not sure where they're going from here. We've already talked about their lack of exciting young players or a deep farm system, but they were also the fourth-oldest roster in baseball last year and had the second-highest payroll in the entire league.

At the end of the day, I think the Giants have put themselves into a corner with bad trades and signings over the past few years, and there was only so much they were going to be able to do to attempt to soften the blow. Yet even with a bar that low, I don't believe the organization even attempted to reach it. I'm not sure you could call this a tank, based on their payroll and lack of prospects or assets, but the Giants surely don't look like a team that has any intentions of winning or even improving the ground they stand on in 2019.

BRET: Yeah, it's certainly more of a middle ground than the teams that have truly taken an axe to their veteran presence, but the sunk money has them in a more precarious position than the teams truly taking the low road. Of course, we also took a hiatus from writing this for a week or so because we were unsure if they'd be able to land Bryce Harper (Ron Howard Voice: they didn't) so that speaks to the overall resources the team has when they choose to use them. It's certainly conceivable that the core of this team could lead them to a near or even slightly above .500 season, which would have the positive effect of likely increasing the trade value of their best chips while also killing their draft position and pool allotment.

It really is the thin edge of a knife that they rest on until this money starts coming off the books in earnest. For the organization's sake, I'll predict a 67-win season and the thirrd overall pick in the draft.

Performance Graphs

2018 Hit List Ranking

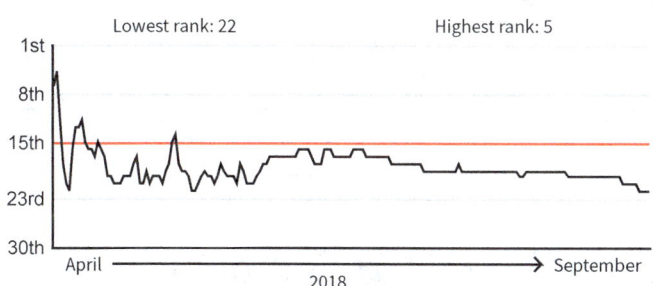

Committed Payroll (in millions)

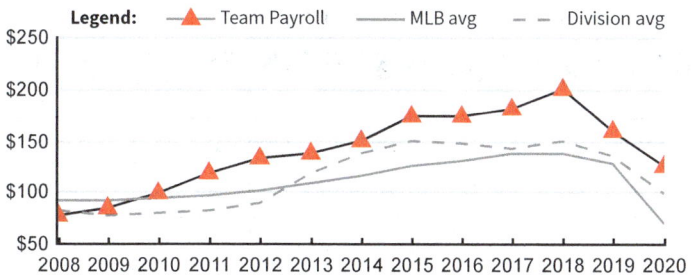

Farm System Ranking

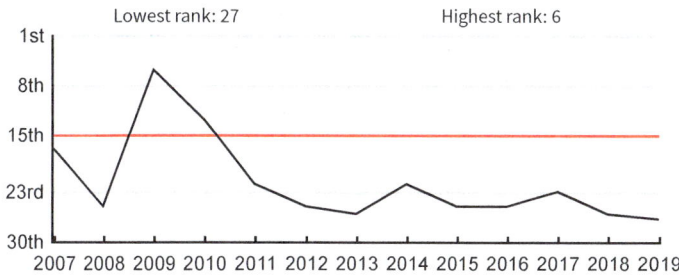

2018 Team Performance

ACTUAL STANDINGS

Team	W	L	Pct
LAN	92	71	.564
COL	91	72	.558
ARI	82	80	.506
SFN	**73**	**89**	**.450**
SDN	66	96	.407

THIRD-ORDER STANDINGS

Team	W	L	Pct
LAN	105	58	.644
COL	88	75	.539
ARI	87	75	.537
SFN	**71**	**91**	**.438**
SDN	66	96	.407

TOP HITTERS

Player	WARP
Brandon Crawford	4
Buster Posey	2.4
Brandon Belt	2.1

TOP PITCHERS

Player	WARP
Derek Holland	2.9
Andrew Suarez	2.3
Reyes Moronta	1.4

VITAL STATISTICS

Statistic Name	Value	Rank
Pythagenpat	.433	21st
Runs Scored per Game	3.72	29th
Runs Allowed per Game	4.31	15th
Deserved Runs Created Plus	81	29th
Deserved Run Average	4.36	16th
Fielding Independent Pitching	3.94	11th
Defensive Efficiency Rating	.707	13th
Batter Age	29.9	30th
Pitcher Age	28.4	16th
Salary	$200.5M	2nd
Marginal $ per Marginal Win	$7.7M	3rd
Disabled List Days	$1,398.0M	25th
$ on DL	28%	28th

2019 Team Projections

PROJECTED STANDINGS

Team	W	L	Pct	+/-
LAN	93	69	.574	+1
COL	84	78	.518	-7
ARI	81	81	.500	-1
SDN	79	83	.487	+13
SFN	**73**	**89**	**.450**	**0**

TOP PROJECTED HITTERS

Player	WARP
Buster Posey	4.6
Brandon Belt	2.6
Brandon Crawford	2.0

TOP PROJECTED PITCHERS

Player	WARP
Madison Bumgarner	1.3
Andrew Suarez	0.7
Will Smith	0.6

FARM SYSTEM REPORT

Top Prospect	Number of Top 101 Prospects
Joey Bart, #2	2

KEY DEDUCTIONS

Player	WARP
Gorkys Hernandez	0.9

KEY ADDITIONS

Player	WARP
Gerardo Parra	0.8
Cameron Maybin	0.5
Drew Pomeranz	0.4
Breyvic Valera	0.4

Team Personnel

President Baseball Operations
Farhan Zaidi

EVP of Baseball Operations
Brian Sabean

SVP, Player Personnel
Dick Tidrow

VP, Assistant General Manager
Jeremy Shelley

VP, Assistant GM, Scouting and International Ops
John Barr

Manager
Bruce Bochy

Oracle Park Stats

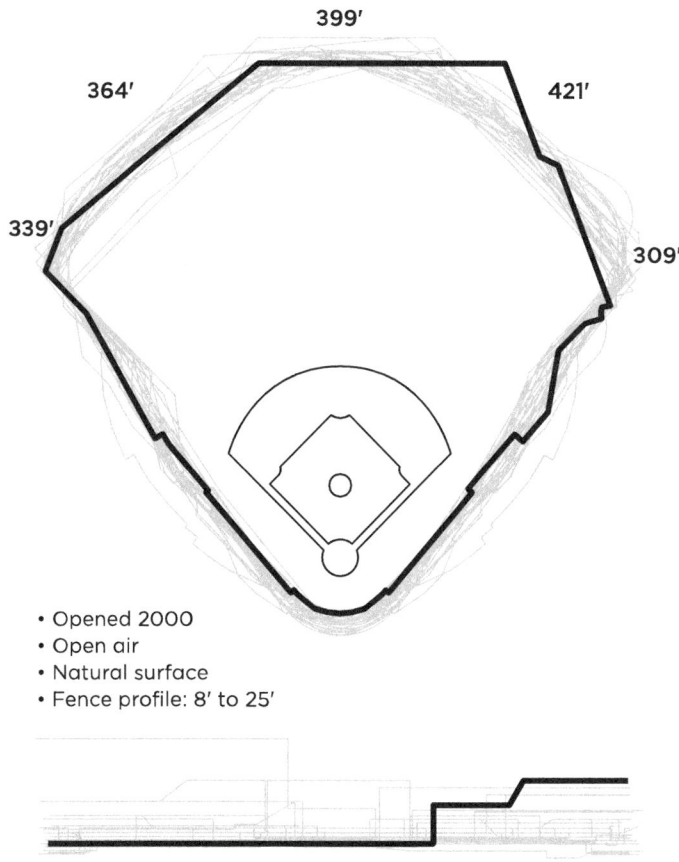

- Opened 2000
- Open air
- Natural surface
- Fence profile: 8' to 25'

Three-Year Park Factors

Runs	Runs/RH	Runs/LH	HR/RH	HR/LH
96	97	94	88	82

Giants Team Analysis

The biggest myth about the Brian Sabean-era Giants was that they weren't into analytics. They were, but it wasn't just the analytics found in a *Bill James Baseball Abstract* that they cared about. When the Giants traded for Jose Vizcaino to be a low-cost stopgap at shortstop in 1996, OBP-fetishists howled (he was worth 1.9 WARP that season). When they signed Rey Sanchez to be a part-time shortstop, the RC/27 crowd shrieked (he was worth 1.4 WARP that season). The Giants understood the importance of defense before dWAR, and it doesn't matter if they were using the eyeball test or scrawling scratch marks on the wall after every catch. They knew that a run saved was roughly as valuable as a run earned, and they built their roster around this truism.

A couple of months after the Giants started playing at Oracle Park in 2000, they noticed something about how the park played, and adjusted their outfield defenses accordingly. Other teams were slower to catch on, and the result was the Giants blowing away the competition in the second half of the season. They soared to the best record in baseball as the pitching staff enjoyed one of the best league-adjusted halves in franchise history. That it wasn't Statcast giving them this information about outfield positioning is beside the point. They were still analyzing the game better than their opponents that season. They were cracking the shell of baseball and feasting on the sweet, sweet nut inside.

And, yes, there were honest-to-goodness stats involved, too. After Aubrey Huff finished seventh in the 2010 NL MVP voting, the Giants' director of quantitative analysis, Yeshayah Goldfarb, explicitly referenced a deep-dive into advanced metrics as the primary reason he was acquired on the cheap. The Giants had a functioning, thriving quantitative analysis department while they were contending, and it helped them win three championships.

So, no, the hiring of a numbers wonk like Farhan Zaidi isn't exactly a revolution in San Francisco. It's more like the organization is taking its array of SETI dishes and pointing them at a different spot in the same sky. The Giants have been into analytics for a long time.

But, holy hell, have they been bad at it for the last couple years.

You can probably find the analogy in your own life. Maybe you were swimming along in your math career, acing algebra and geometry, only to get to calculus and fall into a viper pit. Maybe you followed my path and were a fine baseball player until the kids started throwing hard enough to break bones, at which point you punched the eject button and focused on theater. This is what happened with the Giants, who were analyzing their analytics with analytically sound analysis, and then woke up and found out the teacher was using an entirely different textbook. It was in Cyrillic and kept at the top of a mountain about a day's ride from here. They had no chance.

They've had to readjust before. Back in the early-to-mid-2000s, veterans would stay surprisingly fresh until their late-30s and avoid decline—a testament to hard work and good genes, surely—and the Giants figured out they were often undervalued. They would slap them onto their Winchester Mystery House of a roster, and it worked. Then the Mitchell Report came out, and, that's weird, the strategy stopped working and older veterans weren't as reliable.

When the Giants had to readjust that time, though, the front office found the state of baseball analytics more or less where they left it. Get good players. Develop them if you can, sign them if you have the money, or trade for them if you're creative enough. The Giants lost enough to net the draft picks that became Tim Lincecum, Buster Posey, and Madison Bumgarner, and the Golden Era began. Simple.

That's all still applicable to 2018, but the waterfall of information pouring into every front office changes everything. Now it's all of the above, while also sifting through the data and figuring out how to make your players better, how to make players on other teams better after you bamboozle them away, how to make your prospects better, and how to keep up with your opponents. The same stuff that baseball teams have always done, sure, but it used to be done with bows and arrows, and if you somehow got your hands on a musket, Brad Pitt would play you in the movie. Now it's all F-22 Raptors and nuclear submarines, and the arms race left teams like the Giants behind. They were still evaluating teams the way that they had been for the last two (very successful) decades, and it showed.

Consider the players the Giants employed in 2018. Everyone in the infield was an All-Star at one point. Other than Hunter Pence, everyone was 32 or younger—not exactly pups, but not the age when you expect everyone to fall down an elevator shaft.

They all fell down an elevator shaft.

The Giants finished the second half with a .598 OPS. Their adjusted OPS relative to the league's in the second half was the worst since the 1972 Texas Rangers and the sixth-worst in baseball history. Their .272 on-base percentage in the second half was the eighth worst in baseball history. Everyone was affected. There were no survivors.

Year	Team	2nd half OBP
1908	Superbas	.266
1965	Mets	.268
1972	Rangers	.268
1908	Cardinals	.269
1908	Highlanders	.269
1909	Superbas	.271
1910	Browns	.271
2018	Giants	.272
1910	White Sox	.275
1974	Padres	.278

Now, you can blame a poison cloud hanging over the roster, a contagious malady where everyone starts to tense up just a little bit more because the rest of the team isn't successful, and it all spirals down from there. There had to have been a bit of that going on, you would think.

It can't explain it all away, though. These were all once good players, sometimes as recently as a couple months before. Brandon Crawford had just started the All-Star Game, and Brandon Belt was a candidate for the final vote. But for the third year in a row, the entire Giants lineup absolutely cratered in the second half.

I'm not smart enough to prove this theory myself, but it sure looks like other teams are constantly figuring out the Giants like a collection of *Mike Tyson's Punch Out* opponents. Punch when the ruby flashes. Hit them with a left-right-left combination until you get the TKO. Watch for the uppercut after he blinks. Meanwhile, the Giants were trying to plug a Genesis controller into the NES and saying, "Wait, wait, wait!" They were overmatched.

This theory—this shred of a security blanket—is the only thing keeping me from thinking the Giants will go full Orioles next year. It's not as if Brandon Belt hitting like one of the better first basemen in the National League would be worthy of a feature-length how-did-this-happen breakdown in *Sports Illustrated*. If Evan Longoria suddenly hit at a league-average clip and continued to provide strong defense, it wouldn't make us rethink how we evaluate the game. These would all be the kinds of baseball things that happen in a baseball season with baseball players who are a known quantity. Who were a known quantity, at least.

They just need a different set of eyes. They need several dozen different sets of eyes. The Giants need to rely on analysis, just like they always have. It just needs to be a much, much different analysis. It needs to be the kind of analysis that the cool kids around the league are doing these days. Forget about trying to find the next Max Muncy. They need to find the old Joe Panik.

The need to reevaluate their current roster is of the utmost importance because most of these players are likely to stick around. By the time this article is published, it's possible this will look supremely silly, but I just don't see how this lineup is reinvented. Longoria makes too much money. Posey makes a lot of money and he's coming off hip surgery. Belt makes a lot of money, and his value is unfortunately tethered to his abominable second half. Crawford is a beloved fan favorite, but he has a full no-trade clause and is also compensated fairly.

None of these players will bring back the kinds of prospects needed for a full rebuild. They're all of the "toss in $15 million to get a B- prospect back" variety. It's probably more sensible to see if a new mechanic can get this sucker running again.

Probably not. But nobody expects Zaidi to work miracles in his first offseason, so trying one more time with the bulk of this lineup returning might be the plan. It's also important to note that the Giants are convinced that a full rebuild would set the organization back a decade in the public relations department. They've been one of the top draws in the league, and they're convinced that a screw-this-see-you-in-2022 philosophy would turn the park from a destination into a ghost town. If you think they're being paranoid, just look at the Phillies' attendance over the last five years.

If the Giants are going to threaten .500 next year, they'll be doing it with (mostly) the same hitters because there's no sense paying another team to take them away, get lower-end raffle tickets back, and alienate the casual fan at the same time.

But this has all been about hitting to this point. All the talk about the analytics arms race, all the talk about what has gone wrong since the 2016 All-Star Game has been focused on the lineup. If there was a bright spot to the Giants (and whatever analytics they're using) in 2018, it was the pitching. There aren't a lot of teams that could have survived the loss of Bumgarner, Johnny Cueto, and Jeff Samardzija for the bulk of 2018, but the Giants smoothly adapted. Derek Holland was a revelation, shepherded along nicely in his renaissance season. A couple of disastrous outings made Andrew Suarez's ERA swell, but he was an overwhelming positive for most of the year, a backend rotation piece who made the Giants believe his ceiling might be a little higher than he gets credit for. And, of course, there was Dereck Rodriguez, who probably won't have an ERA under 3.00 again, but gave the organization confidence that they can still scout undervalued contributors with the best of them.

All of this, combined with their rediscovered ability to build a bullpen, should give Zaidi and Giants fans at least some confidence that the organization isn't an unsalvageable Superfund site. They were able to polish pitchers last year. They were keeping up with the arms race in at least one way. They aren't completely hopeless. Mostly hopeless, sure, but don't be a pedant.

This is the state of the 2019 Giants, then. They might have traded Madison Bumgarner by the time you've read this, or they might trade him in July. They might empty the bullpen at the deadline, like the Padres have been so adept at doing in recent years. But you're probably going to see a lot of the same players back. They've likely spent a lot of money on reinforcements by the time you're reading this, whether for the rotation or the outfield or both, and they'll be the butt of a lot of jokes for doing so.

This is all they can do now, though. Figure out how to make their hitters hit. Figure out how to make Oracle Park work for them again. Continue to find and develop pitchers. Build the farm system like they haven't been. Hope they don't threaten 100 losses again, but collect the Posey-high draft picks if they do.

And, above all, hope that they can keep up with the state of baseball analytics in 2019. Hiring an architect away from one of the most advanced organizations in baseball—their blood rival, no less—is a fantastic, necessary start. Just don't be surprised if this new perspective, this new focus on analytics, helps the Giants be much better than you think, much sooner than you think. It's possible that it wasn't the roster or the poor injury luck that was ailing them this whole time. They were just studying for an Analytics 201 midterm while the rest of the league was already finished with their master's thesis, and it's not impossible for them to catch up quickly with the rest of the class.

—Grant Brisbee is a senior writer at SB Nation.

Part 2: Player Analysis

San Francisco Giants 2019

Brandon Belt 1B

Born: 04/20/88 Age: 31 Bats: L Throws: L
Height: 6'4" Weight: 235 Origin: Round 5, 2009 Draft (#147 overall)

YEAR	TEAM	LVL	AGE	PA	R	2B	3B	HR	RBI	BB	K	SB	CS	AVG/OBP/SLG
2016	SFN	MLB	28	655	77	41	8	17	82	104	148	0	4	.275/.394/.474
2017	SFN	MLB	29	451	63	27	3	18	51	66	104	3	2	.241/.355/.469
2018	SFN	MLB	30	456	50	18	2	14	46	49	107	4	0	.253/.342/.414
2019	SFN	MLB	31	529	61	29	3	15	63	63	123	4	2	.253/.348/.427

Breakout: 2% Improve: 33% Collapse: 25% Attrition: 12% MLB: 95%
Comparables: Milton Bradley, Derrek Lee, Ryan Zimmerman

Belt is baseball's ultimate schlimazel. Despite his best efforts to earn love and respect—from a .954 OPS through two months of play to an MLB record 21-pitch plate appearance in May—he's destined for the disabled list and ripe for scapegoating on local radio. This time, it wasn't Belt's proneness to head trauma that snapped his groove. Instead, he left his first June contest and went straight to the hospital for an emergency appendectomy. Belt returned after only two weeks off, but he hit just .203/.280/.290 in his remaining 230 trips to the plate, nursing a bad knee and wasting all the goodwill he'd built up in the spring. He's been a four-win player in his last three healthy seasons, but he's been healthy just twice in his last five. Supporters are certain his luck will turn; detractors will tell you he's a schlimazel for good.

YEAR	TEAM	LVL	AGE	PA	DRC+	VORP	BABIP	BRR	FRAA	WARP
2016	SFN	MLB	28	655	118	37.8	.346	-6.4	1B(151): 0.9, LF(3): 0.0	1.8
2017	SFN	MLB	29	451	110	25.6	.284	0.3	1B(98): 9.0, LF(15): -0.3	2.1
2018	SFN	MLB	30	456	108	14.5	.311	-0.6	1B(104): 9.9, LF(8): 0.3	2.1
2019	SFN	MLB	31	529	112	17.0	.312	-0.6	1B 7	2.6

Brandon Belt, continued

Batted Ball Distribution

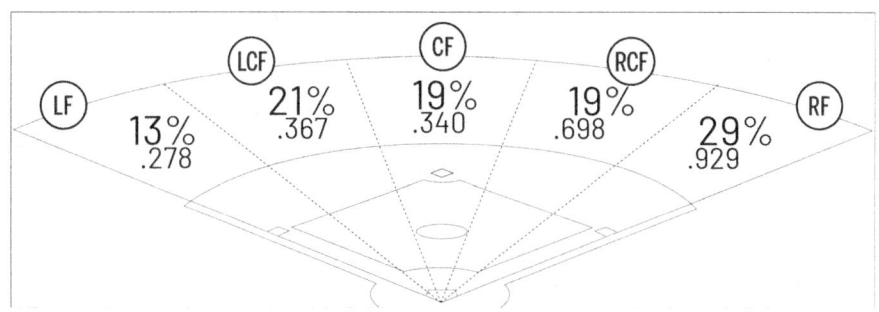

Strike Zone vs LHP

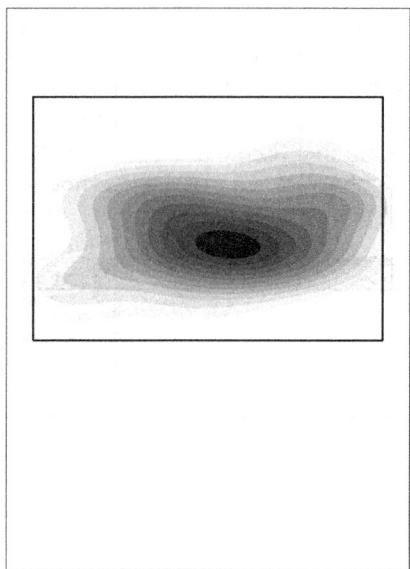

Strike Zone vs RHP

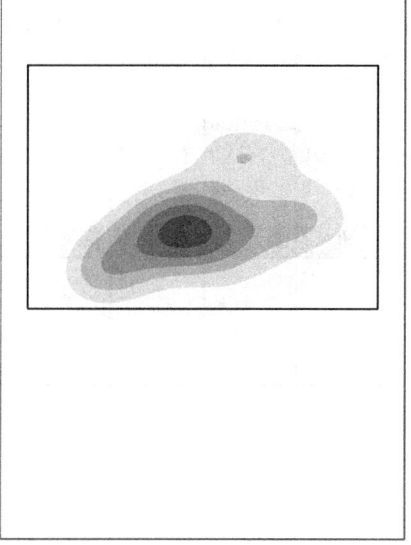

Brandon Crawford SS

Born: 01/21/87 Age: 32 Bats: L Throws: R
Height: 6'2" Weight: 227 Origin: Round 4, 2008 Draft (#117 overall)

YEAR	TEAM	LVL	AGE	PA	R	2B	3B	HR	RBI	BB	K	SB	CS	AVG/OBP/SLG
2016	SFN	MLB	29	623	67	28	11	12	84	57	115	7	0	.275/.342/.430
2017	SFN	MLB	30	570	58	34	1	14	77	42	113	3	5	.253/.305/.403
2018	SFN	MLB	31	594	63	28	2	14	54	50	122	4	5	.254/.325/.394
2019	SFN	MLB	32	573	59	29	3	12	61	49	117	5	4	.254/.323/.392

Breakout: 0% Improve: 36% Collapse: 23% Attrition: 8% MLB: 96%
Comparables: Jhonny Peralta, Asdrubal Cabrera, Stephen Drew

Adjustments and ailments are inevitable parts of a long season, but their impacts don't always jump off the game log like they did for Crawford last year. In the 35 games spanning May 2nd through June 10th, he hit .445/.490/.711, as a tweak to his hand position triggered the best stretch of his career. In the 88 games before and after, he hit a combined .194/.273/.293, nagged by a left knee injury that ruined his balance at the plate. The slump-surge-slump pattern makes it easy to wonder what might have been if Crawford had stayed healthy, but players in their 30s rarely complete a season unscathed. His overall offensive numbers in 2018 were remarkably similar to his 2017 output, and the most likely outcome this year is a repeat of his previous two. Paired with Crawford's perennially exceptional defense, another Gold Glove bid is virtually certain, and he'll vie to start his second straight All-Star Game if he gets hot at the right time again.

YEAR	TEAM	LVL	AGE	PA	DRC+	VORP	BABIP	BRR	FRAA	WARP
2016	SFN	MLB	29	623	94	36.6	.322	-1.8	SS(155): 3.9	2.5
2017	SFN	MLB	30	570	84	24.4	.293	-1.4	SS(138): 4.1	1.7
2018	SFN	MLB	31	594	95	26.5	.303	0.5	SS(146): 15.3	4.0
2019	SFN	MLB	32	573	93	17.7	.305	-1.0	SS 4	2.0

Brandon Crawford, continued

Batted Ball Distribution

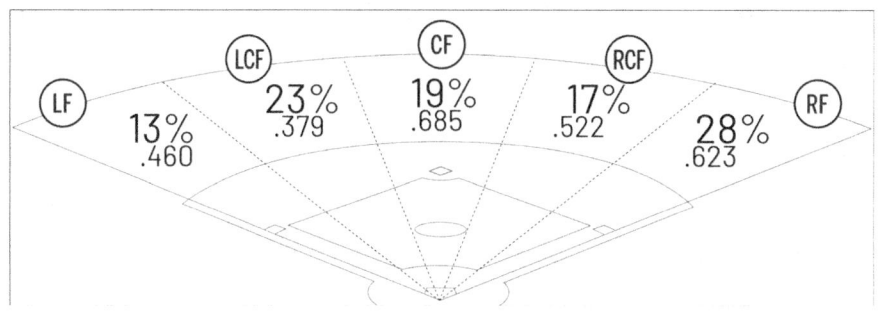

Strike Zone vs LHP

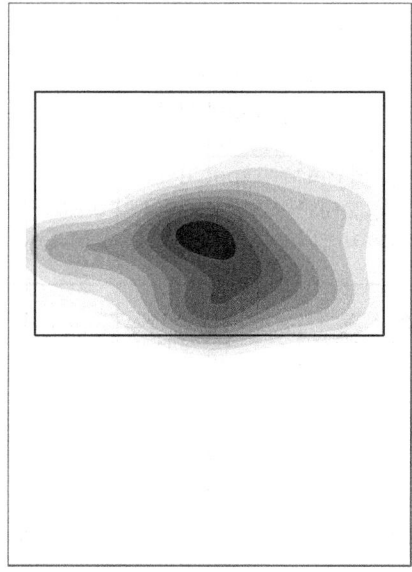

Strike Zone vs RHP

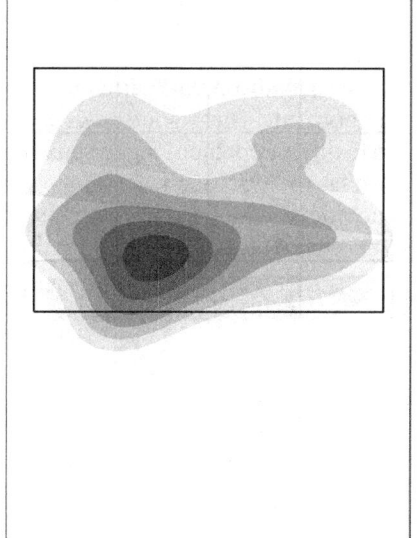

San Francisco Giants 2019

Steven Duggar CF
Born: 11/04/93   Age: 25   Bats: L   Throws: R
Height: 6'2"   Weight: 189   Origin: Round 6, 2015 Draft (#186 overall)

YEAR	TEAM	LVL	AGE	PA	R	2B	3B	HR	RBI	BB	K	SB	CS	AVG/OBP/SLG
2016	SJO	A+	22	311	43	12	4	9	30	44	66	6	7	.284/.386/.462
2016	RIC	AA	22	276	35	16	4	1	24	28	51	9	7	.321/.391/.432
2017	SJO	A+	23	133	22	11	0	4	20	17	42	7	0	.270/.361/.470
2017	SAC	AAA	23	54	7	1	0	2	6	8	12	3	2	.261/.370/.413
2018	SAC	AAA	24	356	52	27	4	4	21	39	103	11	4	.272/.354/.421
2018	SFN	MLB	24	152	20	11	1	2	17	10	44	5	1	.255/.303/.390
2019	SFN	MLB	25	422	45	20	3	8	38	35	122	10	4	.220/.289/.352

Breakout: 18%   Improve: 51%   Collapse: 4%   Attrition: 38%   MLB: 72%
Comparables: Curtis Granderson, Drew Stubbs, Lorenzo Cain

Minor-league scouts occasionally take in big-league contests to restore their perception of the traits and instincts young'uns must develop to succeed. After years of watching veterans on squeaky wheels flunk the eye test in center, Giants fans and Duggar's own teammates needed a similar refresher on major-league-caliber glove work up the middle. Duggar is no Billy Hamilton or Lorenzo Cain, but he's also not late-career Angel Pagan or Denard Span, and he so impressed Madison Bumgarner that the left-hander quipped, "I don't care if he ever gets a hit." That's good news, because the 2015 sixth-rounder will need time to adapt to major-league sequencing, and the torn shoulder labrum that ended his rookie season won't help. Still, Duggar is the most dynamic outfielder borne from the Giants' farm in years, and his range on the pasture might warrant patience with his growing pains at the plate.

YEAR	TEAM	LVL	AGE	PA	DRC+	VORP	BABIP	BRR	FRAA	WARP
2016	SJO	A+	22	311	147	24.5	.346	-2.2	RF(60): 6.3, CF(5): -0.1	1.7
2016	RIC	AA	22	276	148	27.7	.397	1.0	CF(59): 8.4	2.8
2017	SJO	A+	23	133	128	9.9	.386	2.0	RF(22): -2.3, CF(1): -0.2	0.2
2017	SAC	AAA	23	54	92	2.9	.313	0.1	CF(12): 1.7	0.2
2018	SAC	AAA	24	356	103	13.1	.392	-0.1	CF(74): 9.6	1.9
2018	SFN	MLB	24	152	71	8.2	.354	3.6	CF(40): -3.4	0.0
2019	SFN	MLB	25	422	75	4.8	.299	0.6	CF6	1.0

Steven Duggar, continued

Batted Ball Distribution

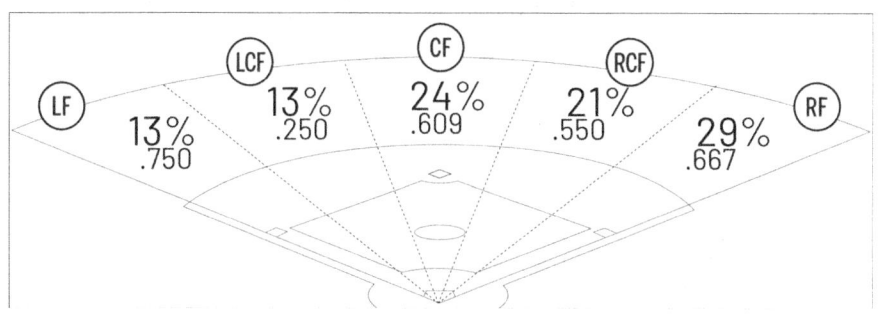

Strike Zone vs LHP

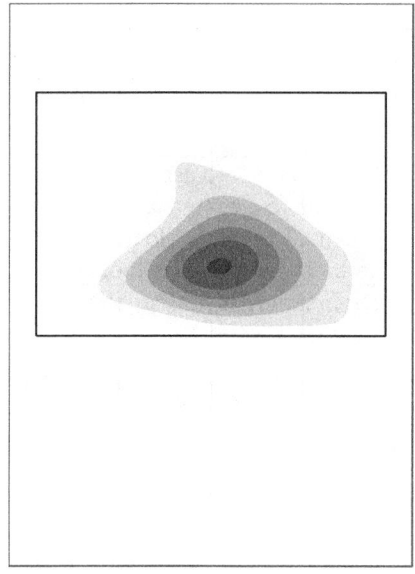

Strike Zone vs RHP

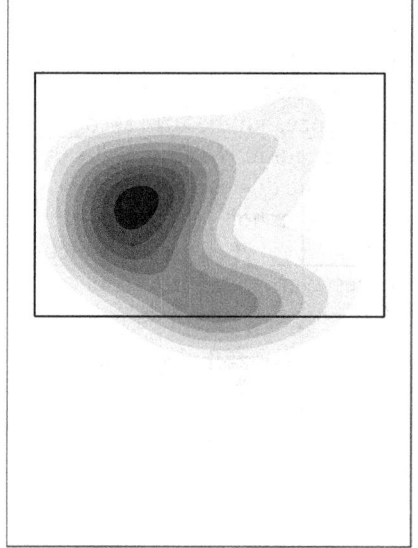

San Francisco Giants 2019

Aramis Garcia C
Born: 01/12/93 Age: 26 Bats: R Throws: R
Height: 6'2" Weight: 220 Origin: Round 2, 2014 Draft (#52 overall)

YEAR	TEAM	LVL	AGE	PA	R	2B	3B	HR	RBI	BB	K	SB	CS	AVG/OBP/SLG
2016	SJO	A+	23	160	20	6	0	2	20	14	42	1	0	.257/.323/.340
2017	SJO	A+	24	347	43	20	1	17	65	15	73	0	0	.272/.314/.497
2017	RIC	AA	24	89	11	12	0	0	8	9	21	0	0	.282/.360/.436
2018	RIC	AA	25	328	36	14	1	11	33	20	76	0	1	.233/.287/.395
2018	SAC	AAA	25	41	5	1	0	0	4	2	12	0	0	.237/.268/.263
2018	SFN	MLB	25	65	8	1	0	4	9	2	31	0	0	.286/.308/.492
2019	SFN	MLB	26	220	21	9	1	7	24	10	65	0	0	.217/.255/.372

Breakout: 9% Improve: 17% Collapse: 3% Attrition: 20% MLB: 30%
Comparables: Cameron Rupp, John Hester, Lucas May

After two years of trudging through the upper minors in hopes of becoming an everyday catcher, Garcia arrived instead as a part-time first baseman who occasionally caught. The late-August promotion was prompted more by injuries than by Garcia's own performance, but the 2014 second-rounder acquitted himself well, putting his plus raw power to use from the jump. On the downside, Garcia struggled to catch up to elevated fastballs, which exposed other holes in his approach. Catchers can take time to blossom with the stick, but at 26, Garcia is stretching the late-bloomer limits. He looks like a tweener, even by backup standards, neither bat-first nor glove-first, offering a little of both but not enough of either.

YEAR	TEAM	P. COUNT	FRM RUNS	BLK RUNS	THRW RUNS	TOT RUNS
2017	RIC	2761	-0.4	0.2	-0.1	-0.7
2018	RIC	9457	13.6	-0.6	-1.5	11.3
2018	SAC	1487	-0.2	0.0	0.0	0.3
2018	SFN	874	0.4	0.3	0.0	0.7
2019	SFN	8044	2.9	-0.7	-0.7	1.4

YEAR	TEAM	LVL	AGE	PA	DRC+	VORP	BABIP	BRR	FRAA	WARP
2016	SJO	A+	23	160	94	4.7	.350	-1.7	C(41): 1.8	0.3
2017	SJO	A+	24	347	115	21.0	.301	-1.3	C(50): 0.7, 1B(17): 0.3	0.8
2017	RIC	AA	24	89	120	6.6	.379	1.0	C(20): -0.5, 1B(2): 0.0	0.5
2018	RIC	AA	25	328	90	10.4	.272	-2.0	C(69): 10.3, 1B(11): -0.5	1.4
2018	SAC	AAA	25	41	60	-1.6	.333	0.3	C(10): 0.5	0.0
2018	SFN	MLB	25	65	55	2.9	.500	0.2	1B(10): -0.6, C(7): 0.7	-0.2
2019	SFN	MLB	26	220	58	-1.3	.273	-0.4	C 0	-0.2

Aramis Garcia, continued

Batted Ball Distribution

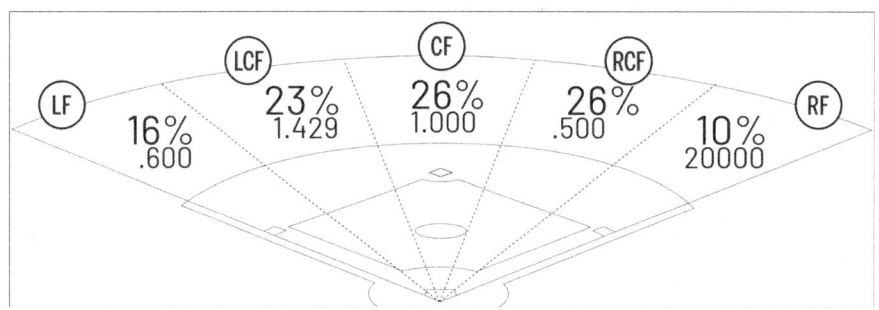

Strike Zone vs LHP   Strike Zone vs RHP

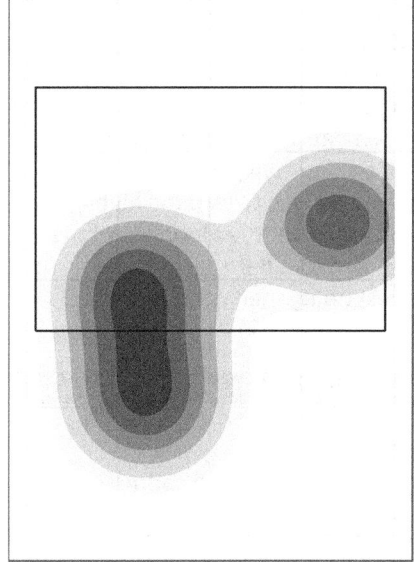 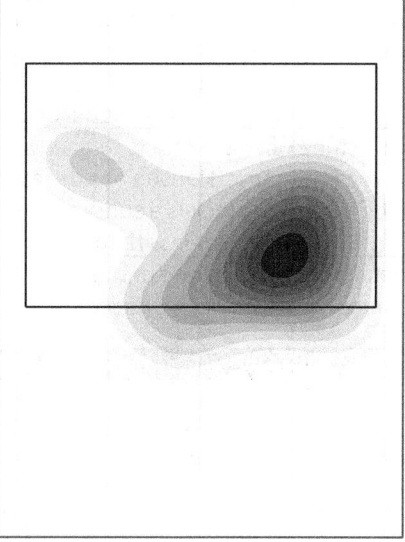

San Francisco Giants 2019

Alen Hanson UT
Born: 10/22/92   Age: 26   Bats: B   Throws: R
Height: 6'0"   Weight: 170   Origin: International Free Agent, 2009

YEAR	TEAM	LVL	AGE	PA	R	2B	3B	HR	RBI	BB	K	SB	CS	AVG/OBP/SLG
2016	IND	AAA	23	478	58	15	7	8	32	32	78	36	15	.266/.318/.389
2016	PIT	MLB	23	33	5	1	0	0	1	2	5	2	1	.226/.273/.258
2017	PIT	MLB	24	59	8	0	2	0	1	2	9	2	1	.193/.220/.263
2017	CHA	MLB	24	175	28	9	1	4	10	10	43	9	2	.231/.276/.375
2018	SAC	AAA	25	71	17	5	1	3	9	8	7	6	1	.403/.479/.661
2018	SFN	MLB	25	310	36	17	5	8	39	9	71	7	3	.252/.274/.425
2019	SFN	MLB	26	112	14	5	1	3	11	6	24	5	2	.243/.288/.398

Breakout: 11%   Improve: 64%   Collapse: 3%   Attrition: 23%   MLB: 94%
Comparables: Cory Spangenberg, Josh Harrison, Devon Travis

Once on the periphery of the league's top 100 prospects, Hanson remains a maddening player with million-dollar tools and ten-cent instincts. The former Pirate is a make-things-happen baserunner, as demonstrated when he scored from first on an errant pickoff attempt in July. That said, he's also a TOOTBLAN connoisseur, prone to running on contact with less than two outs or turning the wrong way after reaching first on a throwing error—mistakes that cost his team in consecutive September games. Those might be excusable if Hanson excelled at getting aboard, but his injudicious approach betrays his innate ability to hit, to the tune of 41 strikeouts to one walk in 56 second-half games. Defensively, it's more of the same: Hanson has the athleticism and arm to lead the highlights, but his internal clock is a sundial, so he's liable to front the blooper reel the next day. The whole is far less than the sum of the five-tool parts, and the same flair that makes Hanson one of the game's flashiest utility men will leave you wondering why he can't be so much more.

YEAR	TEAM	LVL	AGE	PA	DRC+	VORP	BABIP	BRR	FRAA	WARP
2016	IND	AAA	23	478	92	12.3	.307	2.2	2B(67): -8.5, LF(26): -0.3	-0.3
2016	PIT	MLB	23	33	75	-0.4	.269	0.5	2B(8): -0.4	0.0
2017	PIT	MLB	24	59	65	-4.5	.229	-0.9	2B(15): 0.0, RF(2): -0.1	-0.2
2017	CHA	MLB	24	175	66	-0.5	.284	1.7	RF(18): -1.6, 2B(13): -0.1	-0.1
2018	SAC	AAA	25	71	183	14.8	.423	3.2	2B(15): -0.6, SS(2): -0.1	1.1
2018	SFN	MLB	25	310	78	7.2	.303	0.5	2B(45): -1.6, LF(18): -0.8	-0.1
2019	SFN	MLB	26	112	81	1.6	.279	0.5	2B -1, CF 0	0.1

Alen Hanson, continued

Batted Ball Distribution

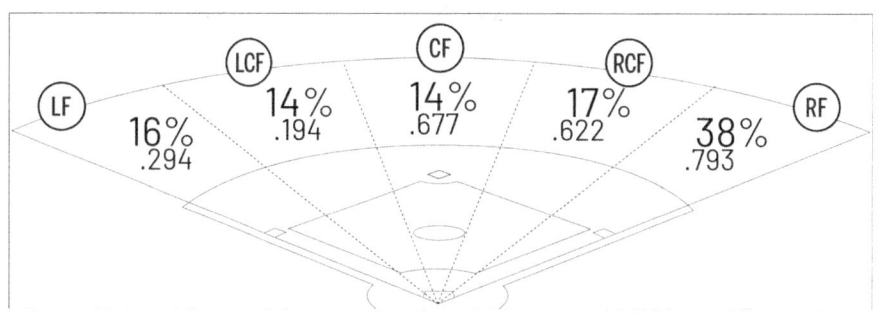

| **Strike Zone vs LHP** | **Strike Zone vs RHP** |

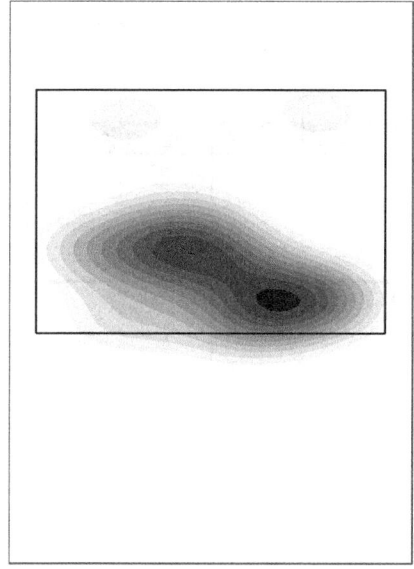
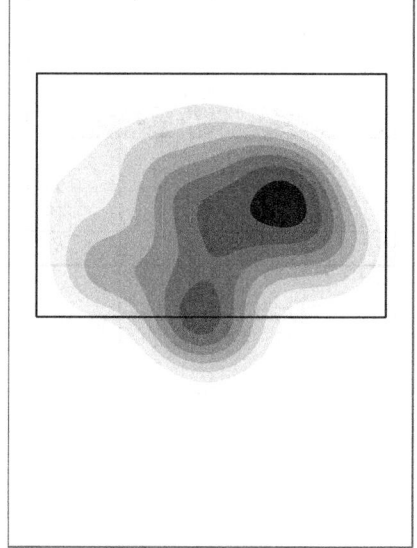

San Francisco Giants 2019

Evan Longoria 3B

Born: 10/07/85 Age: 33 Bats: R Throws: R
Height: 6'1" Weight: 215 Origin: Round 1, 2006 Draft (#3 overall)

YEAR	TEAM	LVL	AGE	PA	R	2B	3B	HR	RBI	BB	K	SB	CS	AVG/OBP/SLG
2016	TBA	MLB	30	685	81	41	4	36	98	42	144	0	3	.273/.318/.521
2017	TBA	MLB	31	677	71	36	2	20	86	46	109	6	1	.261/.313/.424
2018	SFN	MLB	32	512	51	25	4	16	54	22	101	3	1	.244/.281/.413
2019	SFN	MLB	33	565	61	31	3	16	67	42	102	3	1	.259/.319/.425

Breakout: 2% Improve: 23% Collapse: 21% Attrition: 11% MLB: 90%
Comparables: Michael Young, Mike Lamb, Juan Uribe

Longoria's walk rate over the past half-decade tracks the stock price of your favorite office-supply chain in the age of Amazon Prime. No one enjoys seeing the kind folks at Office Depot or Staples lose their jobs, and it's no fun watching a player of Longoria's character have his plate discipline erode. Alas, the trends are largely irreversible, and the third baseman's sinking walk rate has taken his value down with it. Still owed more than $71 million over the next four seasons with a club option for a fifth, the aging Longoria is hurtling toward replacement level. He's a drag on any portfolio, even with the Rays retaining a 15 percent share.

YEAR	TEAM	LVL	AGE	PA	DRC+	VORP	BABIP	BRR	FRAA	WARP
2016	TBA	MLB	30	685	125	41.6	.298	-2.3	3B(152): -5.4	3.6
2017	TBA	MLB	31	677	95	22.4	.282	-1.9	3B(142): 3.8	2.1
2018	SFN	MLB	32	512	89	6.5	.274	-5.2	3B(123): -10.5	-0.5
2019	SFN	MLB	33	565	101	12.3	.291	-0.6	3B -5	0.8

Evan Longoria, continued

Batted Ball Distribution

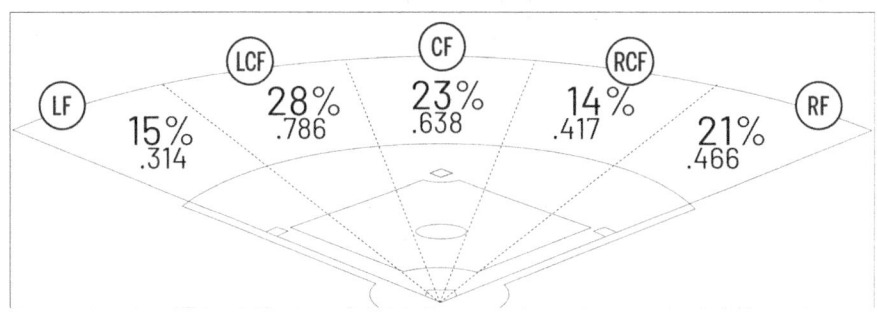

Strike Zone vs LHP

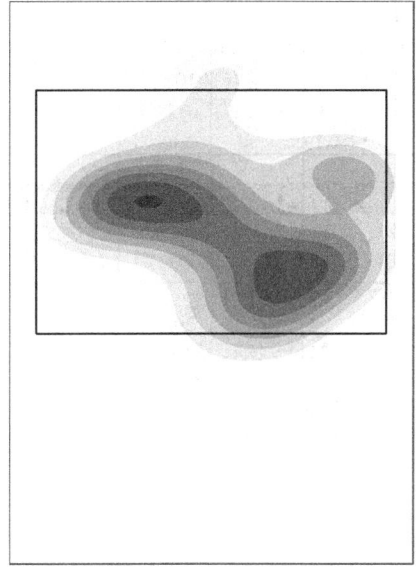

Strike Zone vs RHP

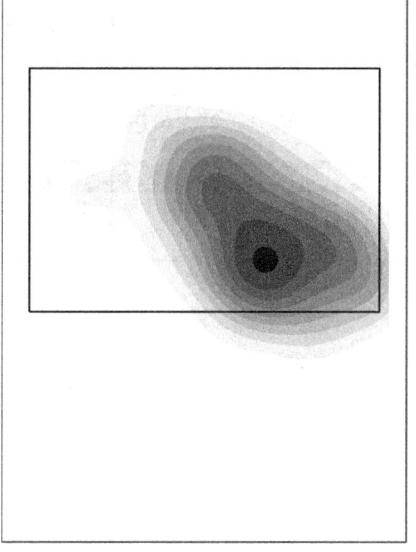

Cameron Maybin OF

Born: 04/04/87 Age: 32 Bats: R Throws: R
Height: 6'3" Weight: 215 Origin: Round 1, 2005 Draft (#10 overall)

YEAR	TEAM	LVL	AGE	PA	R	2B	3B	HR	RBI	BB	K	SB	CS	AVG/OBP/SLG
2016	TOL	AAA	29	100	14	9	0	2	11	14	17	4	1	.188/.310/.365
2016	DET	MLB	29	391	65	14	5	4	43	36	69	15	6	.315/.383/.418
2017	ANA	MLB	30	387	57	19	1	6	22	48	78	29	5	.235/.333/.351
2017	HOU	MLB	30	63	6	1	1	4	13	3	16	4	3	.186/.226/.441
2018	MIA	MLB	31	287	20	12	1	3	20	32	55	8	5	.251/.338/.343
2018	SEA	MLB	31	97	12	2	1	1	8	6	20	2	0	.242/.289/.319
2019	SFN	MLB	32	130	16	6	1	2	12	13	26	6	2	.252/.331/.374

Breakout: 1% Improve: 29% Collapse: 12% Attrition: 14% MLB: 86%
Comparables: Ryan Freel, Jon Jay, Nyjer Morgan

With a long track record of being useful at every aspect of the sport but the part that involves holding a bat, Maybin was a trade deadline acquisition designed to shore up center field. Unfortunately both for him and the Mariners he was still forced, on occasion, to hold the aforementioned bat. A .600 OPS in Seattle coupled with the team's fall from postseason grace led to diminished playing time, until by season's end he was all but replaced by Guillermo Heredia, the very player whose substandard offense he had been brought in to replace. Much like a two-seamer on the hands, life comes at you fast.

YEAR	TEAM	LVL	AGE	PA	DRC+	VORP	BABIP	BRR	FRAA	WARP
2016	TOL	AAA	29	100	102	0.0	.212	0.8	CF(9): 0.3	0.2
2016	DET	MLB	29	391	105	23.9	.383	5.1	CF(91): -1.1	2.0
2017	ANA	MLB	30	387	88	9.9	.289	4.9	LF(45): 2.6, CF(42): 1.5	1.4
2017	HOU	MLB	30	63	87	0.0	.179	-0.4	CF(15): -0.4, LF(5): -0.3	-0.1
2018	MIA	MLB	31	287	89	7.9	.308	-2.7	LF(44): 2.1, CF(30): -0.7	0.3
2018	SEA	MLB	31	97	88	-0.5	.300	-0.2	CF(20): -1.6, LF(12): 0.4	0.0
2019	SFN	MLB	32	130	92	3.8	.301	0.5	CF 0, LF 1	0.5

Cameron Maybin, continued

Batted Ball Distribution

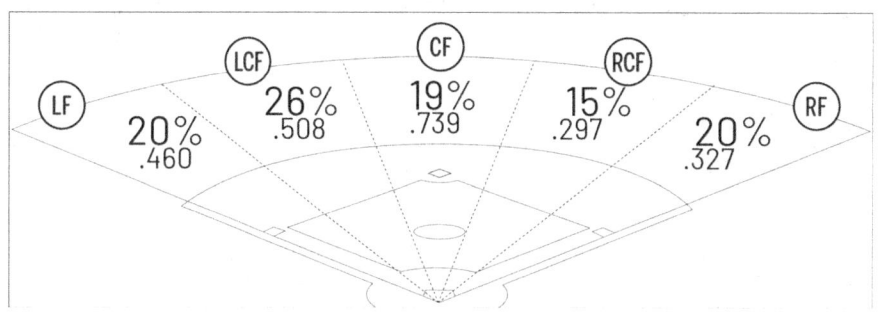

Strike Zone vs LHP

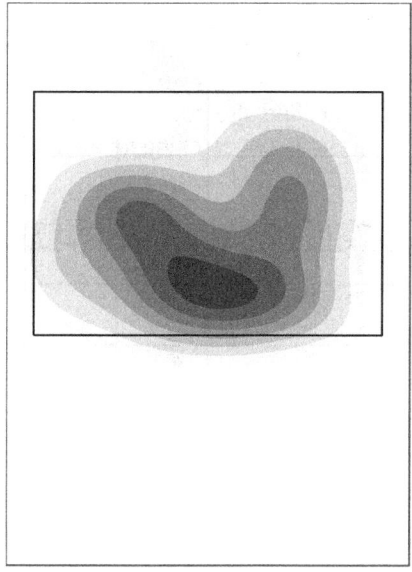

Strike Zone vs RHP

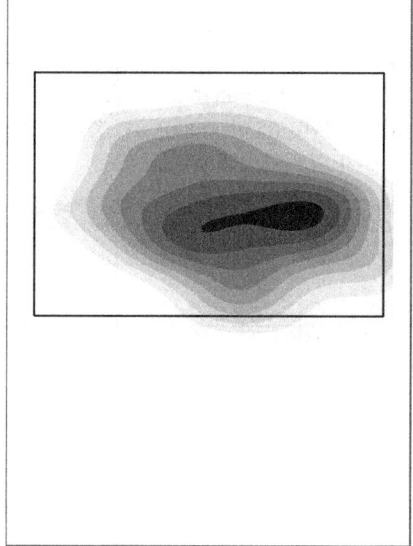

Joe Panik 2B

Born: 10/30/90 Age: 28 Bats: L Throws: R
Height: 6'1" Weight: 200 Origin: Round 1, 2011 Draft (#29 overall)

YEAR	TEAM	LVL	AGE	PA	R	2B	3B	HR	RBI	BB	K	SB	CS	AVG/OBP/SLG
2016	SFN	MLB	25	526	67	21	7	10	62	50	47	5	0	.239/.315/.379
2017	SFN	MLB	26	573	60	28	5	10	53	46	54	4	1	.288/.347/.421
2018	SFN	MLB	27	392	38	14	1	4	24	26	30	4	2	.254/.307/.332
2019	SFN	MLB	28	479	55	23	3	9	44	37	51	4	1	.262/.325/.391

Breakout: 0% Improve: 40% Collapse: 8% Attrition: 9% MLB: 96%
Comparables: Nellie Fox, Felix Millan, Johnny Ray

On Opening Day of the 2018 season, Panik homered and the Giants won 1-0. The next day, Panik homered again and the Giants won 1-0 once more. Beyond their historical significance—no team had ever won back-to-back games on the same player's solo shots—those swings offered hope that the National League's feistiest contact hitter might have developed a power stroke to augment his game. Not so. Addled by a torn thumb ligament and a groin strain, Panik clubbed only two more homers the rest of the way, scuffling through the worst offensive season of his career. Panik's appeal used to be his stability—you could pencil him in for two WARP at the keystone and worry about everything else. But putting the ball in play ain't what it used to be, and after four years of rolling with the whims of the BABIP gods, he enters his late-20s searching for a sturdier foundation at the plate.

YEAR	TEAM	LVL	AGE	PA	DRC+	VORP	BABIP	BRR	FRAA	WARP
2016	SFN	MLB	25	526	85	13.2	.245	1.3	2B(126): 12.7	2.1
2017	SFN	MLB	26	573	100	27.2	.301	0.9	2B(137): -7.5	1.1
2018	SFN	MLB	27	392	86	1.3	.265	1.0	2B(94): 4.3, 1B(1): 0.1	1.1
2019	SFN	MLB	28	479	95	15.2	.276	-0.2	2B 2	1.5

Joe Panik, continued

Batted Ball Distribution

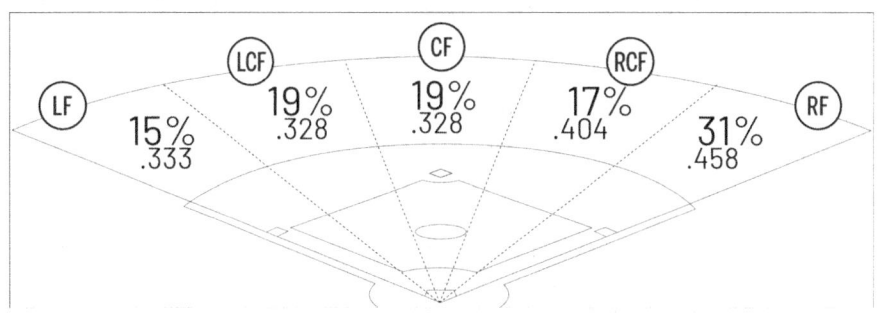

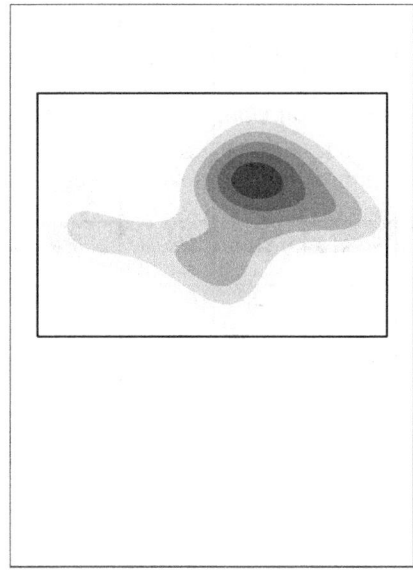

Strike Zone vs LHP

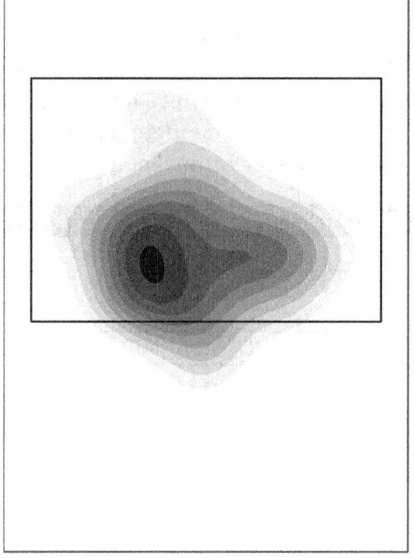

Strike Zone vs RHP

Gerardo Parra   RF

Born: 05/06/87   Age: 32   Bats: L   Throws: L
Height: 5'11"   Weight: 210   Origin: International Free Agent, 2004

YEAR	TEAM	LVL	AGE	PA	R	2B	3B	HR	RBI	BB	K	SB	CS	AVG/OBP/SLG
2016	COL	MLB	29	381	45	27	3	7	39	9	73	6	4	.253/.271/.399
2017	COL	MLB	30	425	56	24	1	10	71	20	67	2	5	.309/.341/.452
2018	COL	MLB	31	443	52	17	0	6	53	32	75	11	4	.284/.342/.372
2019	SFN	MLB	32	310	32	16	2	5	31	18	56	5	3	.266/.314/.388

Breakout: 1%   Improve: 31%   Collapse: 11%   Attrition: 14%   MLB: 88%
Comparables: Bama Rowell, Johnny Moore, Mike McCormick

It's never a great thing when a player's Instagram feed is the most popular thing about him, and yet there we were with El Yolo in 2018. In a move that was perhaps over-reactive to Parra's scorching second half, and one that was definitely in spite of ample young organizational depth, Colorado turned over a set of everyday outfield keys to the career second-divisional stalwart. The bat didn't hold up to the increased exposure, but a draw-down to proper part-time status down the stretch resulted in some positively sublime pinch-hitting efforts. And a year after his bat bounced like a dead cat, it was his glove's turn. With the pinch-hitting prowess and some sneaky value added on the basepaths, he wound up producing a half-decent two-win season, public perception be damned. It wasn't enough to coax the club into exercising his $12.5 million team option, however, so he'll need to reacquaint himself with sea level once again.

YEAR	TEAM	LVL	AGE	PA	DRC+	VORP	BABIP	BRR	FRAA	WARP
2016	COL	MLB	29	381	66	-1.7	.297	-1.1	LF(60): 1.8, 1B(19): 0.4	-0.8
2017	COL	MLB	30	425	99	10.2	.343	-2.5	LF(82): 3.6, RF(22): -0.1	1.1
2018	COL	MLB	31	443	96	10.9	.334	3.3	LF(111): 6.8, RF(10): 1.9	2.1
2019	SFN	MLB	32	310	89	5.7	.309	-0.3	LF 2, RF 0	0.8

Gerardo Parra, continued

Batted Ball Distribution

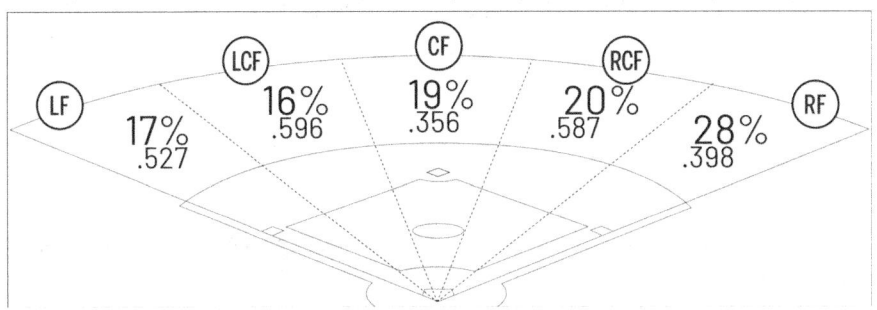

Strike Zone vs LHP

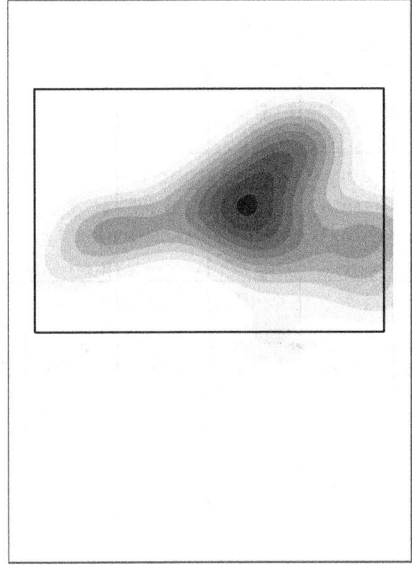

Strike Zone vs RHP

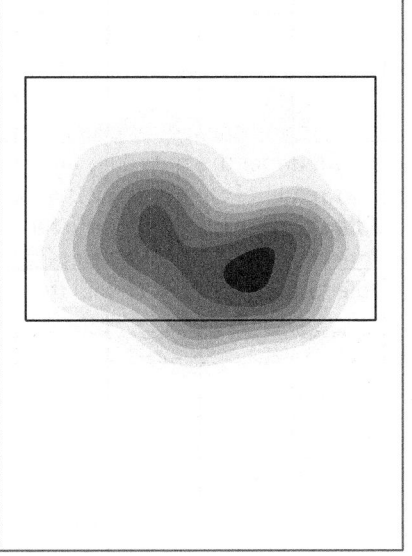

Buster Posey C

Born: 03/27/87   Age: 32   Bats: R   Throws: R
Height: 6'1"   Weight: 210   Origin: Round 1, 2008 Draft (#5 overall)

YEAR	TEAM	LVL	AGE	PA	R	2B	3B	HR	RBI	BB	K	SB	CS	AVG/OBP/SLG
2016	SFN	MLB	29	614	82	33	2	14	80	64	68	6	1	.288/.362/.434
2017	SFN	MLB	30	568	62	34	0	12	67	61	66	6	1	.320/.400/.462
2018	SFN	MLB	31	448	47	22	1	5	41	45	53	3	2	.284/.359/.382
2019	SFN	MLB	32	556	71	29	2	10	53	63	72	4	1	.286/.372/.416

Breakout: 0%   Improve: 27%   Collapse: 24%   Attrition: 9%   MLB: 95%
Comparables: Yadier Molina, Victor Martinez, Jonathan Lucroy

While the shoulders and arms control the bat, the back hip is the most important joint in hitting. Any weakness there, any decrease in mobility, can sap a hitter's power and prevent him from staying back against offspeed and spin. In Posey's case, it was both: A torn labrum and microfracture turned the one-time slugger into a slapper who could barely threaten the gaps, much less the fence. Despite the pain and the wear, Posey remained unimpressed with the fastest of fastballs, but sliders and changeups exposed his wobbly base. By late August, he relented and went under the knife. Like any major surgery, hip procedures are risky, and Posey's readiness for Opening Day is no sure thing—it falls squarely in the middle of his six-to-eight-month recovery estimate. Still, if the former MVP can restore even a fraction of his vintage power without the injury rendering him unable to catch, he could rejoin the National League's elite.

YEAR	TEAM	P. COUNT	FRM RUNS	BLK RUNS	THRW RUNS	TOT RUNS
2016	SFN	17017	28.9	2.0	2.2	32.9
2017	SFN	13474	4.8	0.2	2.3	7.4
2018	SFN	12224	0.9	0.7	0.1	2.0
2019	SFN	15477	7.9	1.1	1.1	10.0

YEAR	TEAM	LVL	AGE	PA	DRC+	VORP	BABIP	BRR	FRAA	WARP
2016	SFN	MLB	29	614	109	40.5	.303	-3.3	C(123): 37.0, 1B(15): -0.7	6.8
2017	SFN	MLB	30	568	129	50.2	.347	-1.5	C(99): 7.0, 1B(38): 3.5	5.2
2018	SFN	MLB	31	448	107	20.1	.316	-1.3	C(88): 0.1, 1B(13): 1.5	2.4
2019	SFN	MLB	32	556	119	35.3	.316	-0.6	C 8, 1B 2	4.6

Buster Posey, continued

Batted Ball Distribution

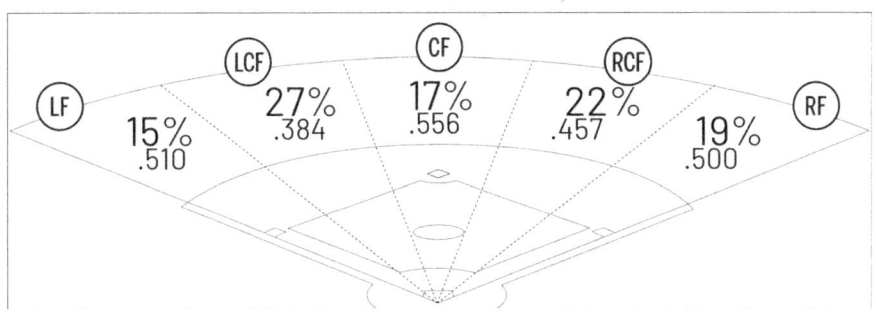

Strike Zone vs LHP	**Strike Zone vs RHP**

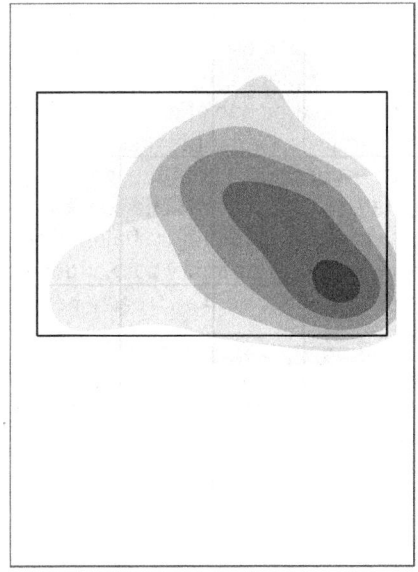 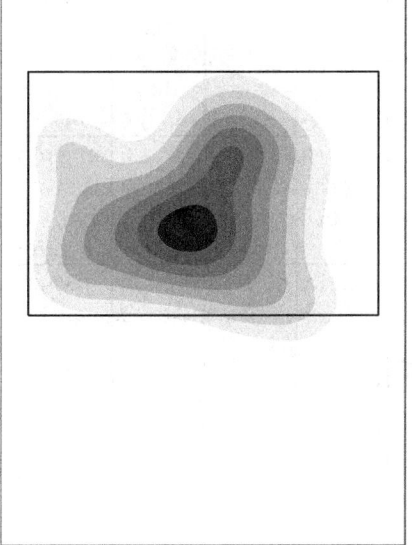

San Francisco Giants 2019

Pablo Sandoval 3B

Born: 08/11/86   Age: 32   Bats: B   Throws: R
Height: 5'11"   Weight: 268   Origin: International Free Agent, 2003

YEAR	TEAM	LVL	AGE	PA	R	2B	3B	HR	RBI	BB	K	SB	CS	AVG/OBP/SLG
2016	BOS	MLB	29	7	0	0	0	0	0	1	4	0	0	.000/.143/.000
2017	BOS	MLB	30	108	10	2	0	4	12	8	24	0	1	.212/.269/.354
2017	PAW	AAA	30	81	7	3	0	1	4	4	16	0	0	.221/.259/.299
2017	SAC	AAA	30	37	4	1	0	1	3	5	3	0	0	.207/.324/.345
2017	SFN	MLB	30	171	17	9	0	5	20	8	29	0	0	.225/.263/.375
2018	SFN	MLB	31	252	22	10	1	9	40	19	52	0	0	.248/.310/.417
2019	SFN	MLB	32	146	15	6	1	4	16	11	30	0	0	.241/.301/.391

Breakout: 3%   Improve: 32%   Collapse: 20%   Attrition: 11%   MLB: 91%
Comparables: Casey McGehee, B.J. Surhoff, Russ Wrightstone

When the Red Sox released Sandoval in July 2017, his career hung in the balance, imperiled by poor conditioning, a shoulder injury that sapped his power and a bad-ball approach known to accelerate the expiration dates of major-league bats. Granted a second chance by his first employer, he came to Spring Training looking slimmer, swinging easier and, most notably, swinging less. Players rarely make a mid-career U-turn at the plate, but Sandoval—once one of the league's leading first-pitch-hackers—became one of the most willing to let the 0-0 offering go by. In 252 plate appearances, he put the first pitch in play only four times. His 1.6 percent was a stark contrast to both the league average of 10.9 percent and his own career rate of 15.1 percent. The result was a productive corner-infield reserve, well worth the league-minimum balance of a contract on the Red Sox' books through 2019. A hamstring injury cut Sandoval's season two months short, but assuming he keeps the patient approach, he'll be a fine fill-in at first and third again this year.

YEAR	TEAM	LVL	AGE	PA	DRC+	VORP	BABIP	BRR	FRAA	WARP
2016	BOS	MLB	29	7	69	-1.0	.000	0.0	3B(2): 0.1	0.0
2017	BOS	MLB	30	108	81	-1.9	.236	-0.2	3B(29): -1.4, 2B(1): 0.0	0.0
2017	PAW	AAA	30	81	70	-2.8	.267	-0.5	3B(15): -1.6	-0.3
2017	SAC	AAA	30	37	79	1.3	.185	-0.1	3B(7): 1.2	0.1
2017	SFN	MLB	30	171	80	-0.8	.242	-0.4	3B(38): -2.6, 1B(9): -0.1	-0.2
2018	SFN	MLB	31	252	96	1.4	.282	-2.8	3B(36): -1.8, 1B(24): -1.4	-0.1
2019	SFN	MLB	32	146	85	0.8	.283	-0.2	3B -1, 1B 0	-0.1

Pablo Sandoval, continued

Batted Ball Distribution

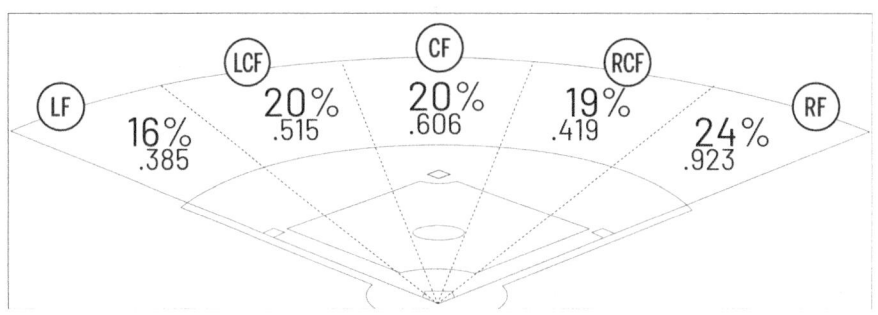

Strike Zone vs LHP

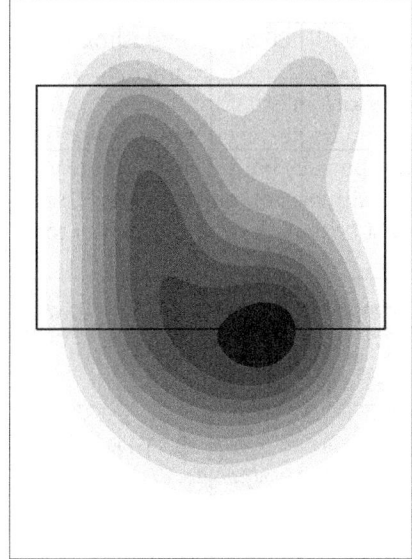

Strike Zone vs RHP

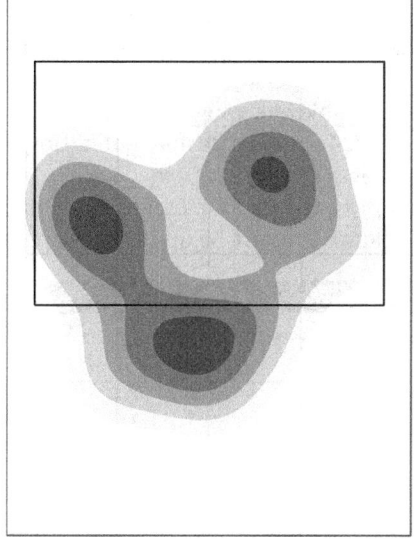

Austin Slater OF

Born: 12/13/92 Age: 26 Bats: R Throws: R
Height: 6'2" Weight: 197 Origin: Round 8, 2014 Draft (#238 overall)

YEAR	TEAM	LVL	AGE	PA	R	2B	3B	HR	RBI	BB	K	SB	CS	AVG/OBP/SLG
2016	RIC	AA	23	172	20	8	1	5	25	24	36	6	1	.317/.413/.490
2016	SAC	AAA	23	278	36	12	0	13	42	33	53	2	6	.298/.381/.506
2017	SAC	AAA	24	206	28	12	0	5	27	15	39	4	3	.321/.377/.467
2017	SFN	MLB	24	127	15	3	1	3	16	8	29	0	0	.282/.339/.402
2018	SAC	AAA	25	223	32	24	2	5	32	21	39	8	2	.344/.417/.564
2018	SFN	MLB	25	225	21	6	1	1	23	20	69	7	0	.251/.333/.307
2019	SFN	MLB	26	402	44	18	2	10	44	34	97	7	2	.247/.318/.392

Breakout: 15% Improve: 42% Collapse: 11% Attrition: 23% MLB: 80%
Comparables: John Bowker, Shin-Soo Choo, Wladimir Balentien

There's some benefit to zagging while everyone zigs, but Slater's batted-ball profile tests the limits of bucking conventional wisdom. As nearly all his brethren aim to lift the ball pull-side, Slater doggedly filets even the meatiest of pitches the other way. He sent 36 percent of his balls in play to the opposite field, more than any other right-handed hitter with 200 or more trips to the plate. His 63.1 percent ground-ball rate led the same group, as did his 3.9 grounders-per-fly. That spray chart made the former Stanford standout unshiftable, allowing him to bat .317 on grounders despite not being very fast and .724 on liners despite not hitting them especially hard. The downside is evident in Slater's ISO, the lowest of anyone with his volume of at-bats. That simply won't do for a corner outfielder or first baseman, relegating Slater to backup duty until he updates his approach.

YEAR	TEAM	LVL	AGE	PA	DRC+	VORP	BABIP	BRR	FRAA	WARP
2016	RIC	AA	23	172	163	19.5	.387	1.1	CF(33): -10.0, LF(7): -0.4	0.3
2016	SAC	AAA	23	278	143	26.1	.335	-0.5	LF(48): 0.4, CF(15): -1.3	1.4
2017	SAC	AAA	24	206	119	9.1	.380	-2.7	RF(22): -0.9, LF(17): -0.1	0.5
2017	SFN	MLB	24	127	84	4.9	.353	0.2	LF(30): -1.0, RF(3): -0.2	0.0
2018	SAC	AAA	25	223	164	22.2	.405	1.4	RF(29): 0.6, 1B(13): -0.1	1.8
2018	SFN	MLB	25	225	64	1.8	.377	1.3	LF(25): 1.8, 1B(21): 0.1	-0.2
2019	SFN	MLB	26	402	97	10.7	.311	0.2	RF -6	0.3

Austin Slater, continued

Batted Ball Distribution

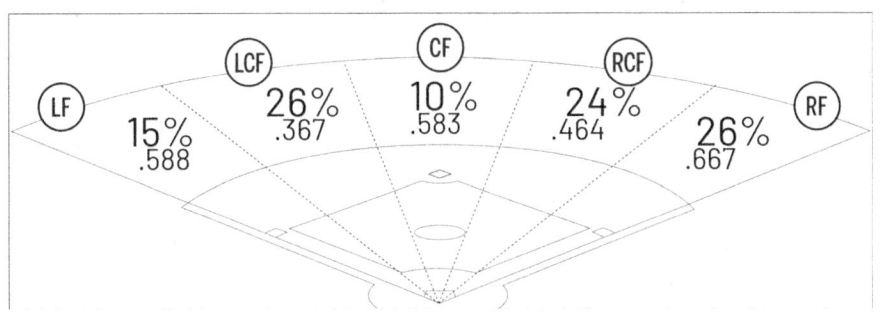

Strike Zone vs LHP

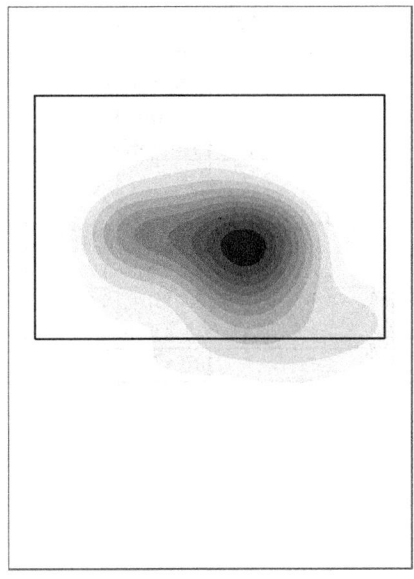

Strike Zone vs RHP

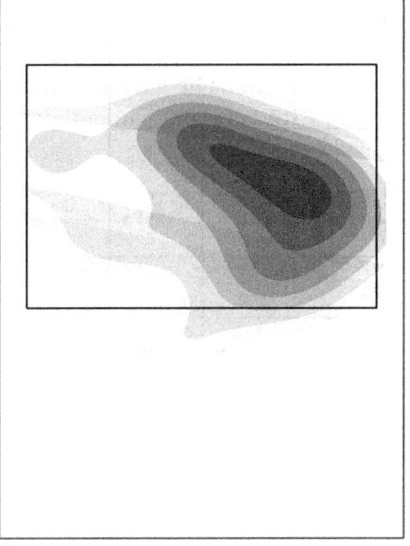

Yangervis Solarte INF
Born: 07/03/87   Age: 31   Bats: B   Throws: R
Height: 5'11"   Weight: 205   Origin: International Free Agent, 2005

YEAR	TEAM	LVL	AGE	PA	R	2B	3B	HR	RBI	BB	K	SB	CS	AVG/OBP/SLG
2016	SDN	MLB	28	443	55	26	1	15	71	30	63	1	1	.286/.341/.467
2017	SDN	MLB	29	512	49	21	0	18	64	37	61	3	0	.255/.314/.416
2018	TOR	MLB	30	506	50	20	0	17	54	31	72	1	3	.226/.277/.378
2019	SFN	MLB	31	253	26	12	1	7	29	17	36	1	1	.255/.312/.407

Breakout: 3%   Improve: 35%   Collapse: 14%   Attrition: 8%   MLB: 96%
Comparables: Alberto Callaspo, Pie Traynor, Martin Prado

In ways both bittersweet and sour, Solarte picked up the mantle left by fan favorite Munenori Kawasaki upon his arrival to Rogers Centre in the spring of 2018. His infectious energy spilled out of the dugout, manifesting in toe-tapping stretches, spontaneous drumming and something that he dubbed "El Sexy Time." That kind of pure joy should permeate what is, at its core, still a simple game, but Solarte began to mirror Kawasaki in less-delightful ways as the season started to pick up. Once a promising cleanup hitter, his approach waned in his age-30 season and, as a result, saw the first below-average offensive season of his career. He's also entering the phase of his career where defensive utility is something he'll have to fight for on a yearly basis, and Solarte lost that battle in 2018 as his hot corner defense slowly erodes into more gaffes than highlight-reel head-turners.

YEAR	TEAM	LVL	AGE	PA	DRC+	VORP	BABIP	BRR	FRAA	WARP
2016	SDN	MLB	28	443	109	24.9	.306	-2.2	3B(95): 6.1, 2B(15): 0.9	2.5
2017	SDN	MLB	29	512	98	16.9	.258	0.5	2B(79): -3.4, SS(28): -1.8	1.2
2018	TOR	MLB	30	506	83	-7.8	.233	-3.4	3B(83): 0.1, 2B(28): -0.5	0.3
2019	SFN	MLB	31	253	87	3.2	.274	-0.4	3B 0, SS -1	0.2

Yangervis Solarte, continued

Batted Ball Distribution

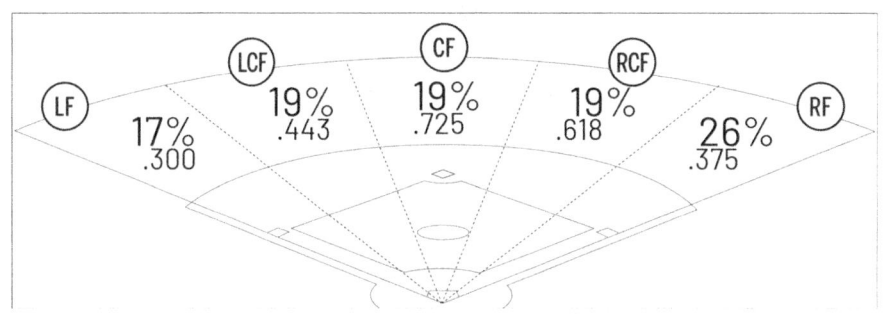

Strike Zone vs LHP   **Strike Zone vs RHP**

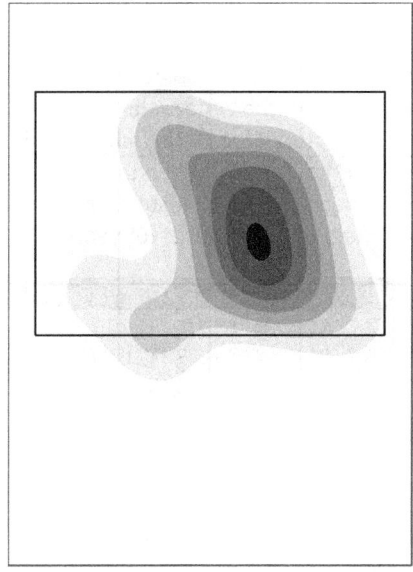 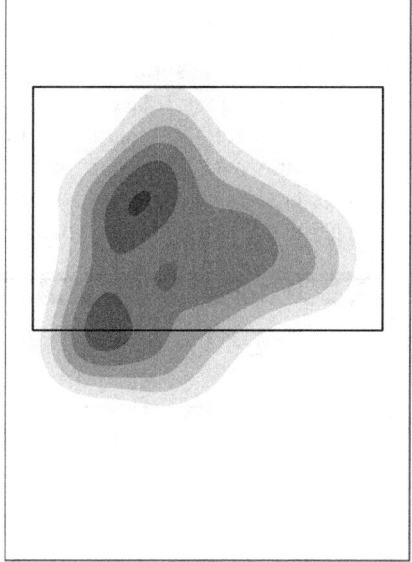

Breyvic Valera UT

Born: 01/08/92   Age: 27   Bats: B   Throws: R
Height: 5'11"   Weight: 160   Origin: International Free Agent, 2010

YEAR	TEAM	LVL	AGE	PA	R	2B	3B	HR	RBI	BB	K	SB	CS	AVG/OBP/SLG
2016	SFD	AA	24	192	16	5	1	0	12	9	18	3	1	.258/.289/.298
2016	MEM	AAA	24	257	32	14	1	0	31	31	22	8	4	.341/.417/.415
2017	MEM	AAA	25	470	68	22	6	8	41	38	34	11	11	.314/.368/.450
2017	SLN	MLB	25	11	0	0	0	0	0	1	0	0	0	.100/.182/.100
2018	LAN	MLB	26	34	4	0	0	0	4	4	4	0	0	.172/.273/.172
2018	OKL	AAA	26	223	36	8	2	6	25	21	20	4	6	.284/.350/.433
2018	NOR	AAA	26	160	14	6	2	3	14	16	14	3	2	.229/.310/.364
2018	BAL	MLB	26	41	4	0	1	0	4	3	9	1	0	.286/.325/.343
2019	SFN	MLB	27	123	13	5	1	2	12	8	16	2	1	.265/.317/.381

Breakout: 6%   Improve: 29%   Collapse: 0%   Attrition: 23%   MLB: 50%
Comparables: Jeff Keppinger, Eric Sogard, Jarrett Hoffpauir

A long-time Cardinals prospect, Valera was picked up by the Dodgers this season as a stopgap measure after the Corey Seager injury, and then flipped to the O's in the Machado trade. Here are three interesting things about Valera, a switch-hitting infielder: 1) 10 separate times, at levels ranging from rookie ball to Triple-A, he has had a higher BB% than K%. 2) He hails from the Venezuelan state of Carabobo, or in literal translation from Spanish, "stupid face." 3) While candid photos are fine, every single posed photograph that has ever been taken of Breyvic Valera has made him look like a combination of Frankenstein's monster and a cliff face that has lured unsuspecting hikers to their deaths for years.

YEAR	TEAM	LVL	AGE	PA	DRC+	VORP	BABIP	BRR	FRAA	WARP
2016	SFD	AA	24	192	81	-2.0	.282	0.8	SS(26): 1.1, 2B(15): 1.2	0.0
2016	MEM	AAA	24	257	141	28.5	.370	1.6	2B(32): -1.9, 3B(21): 0.6	1.6
2017	MEM	AAA	25	470	117	31.9	.324	1.5	2B(78): -1.3, LF(18): 0.5	1.9
2017	SLN	MLB	25	11	86	-1.3	.100	0.0	2B(3): -0.2	0.0
2018	LAN	MLB	26	34	87	-1.3	.200	0.3	2B(5): -0.4, 3B(3): -0.1	0.0
2018	OKL	AAA	26	223	105	12.6	.290	0.7	SS(25): -0.4, 2B(16): -0.8	0.8
2018	NOR	AAA	26	160	108	4.3	.234	-1.8	2B(25): 3.0, LF(7): -0.1	0.5
2018	BAL	MLB	26	41	89	0.9	.357	0.1	2B(11): -1.3, SS(2): -0.1	-0.1
2019	SFN	MLB	27	123	97	4.0	.289	-0.2	2B -1, SS 0	0.4

Breyvic Valera, continued

Batted Ball Distribution

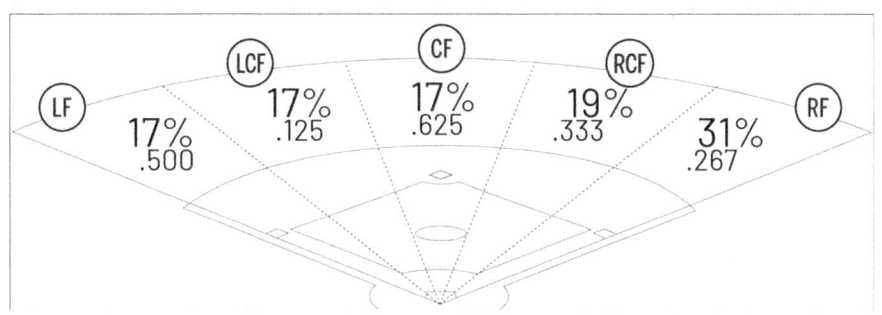

Strike Zone vs LHP

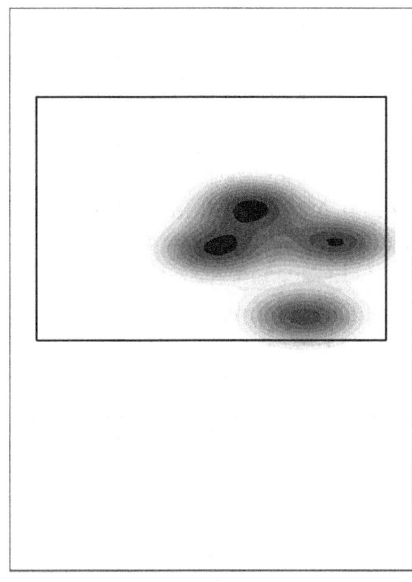

Strike Zone vs RHP

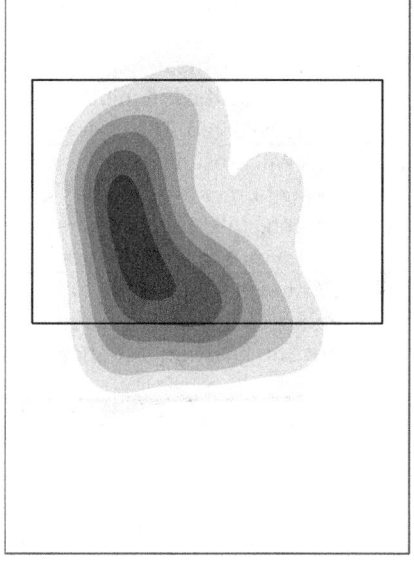

San Francisco Giants 2019

Mac Williamson LF

Born: 07/15/90   Age: 28   Bats: R   Throws: R
Height: 6'4"   Weight: 237   Origin: Round 3, 2012 Draft (#115 overall)

YEAR	TEAM	LVL	AGE	PA	R	2B	3B	HR	RBI	BB	K	SB	CS	AVG/OBP/SLG
2016	SAC	AAA	25	226	35	14	0	11	42	12	53	2	1	.269/.314/.495
2016	SFN	MLB	25	127	14	3	0	6	15	13	35	0	1	.223/.315/.411
2017	SAC	AAA	26	382	54	21	0	14	50	25	100	4	1	.244/.301/.423
2017	SFN	MLB	26	73	8	2	0	3	6	5	25	1	1	.235/.288/.397
2018	SFN	MLB	27	105	14	4	0	4	11	11	27	1	1	.213/.295/.383
2018	SAC	AAA	27	215	31	7	1	13	44	23	44	1	0	.269/.372/.533
2019	SFN	MLB	28	338	38	14	1	12	39	24	90	2	1	.221/.284/.390

Breakout: 7%   Improve: 18%   Collapse: 14%   Attrition: 25%   MLB: 54%
Comparables: John Rodriguez, Todd Linden, Matt Tuiasosopo

Blessed with the most raw power in the organization, Williamson struggled to actualize his strength because of subpar contact rates and a propensity to pound the ball into the ground. While at Triple-A Sacramento in 2017, journeyman catcher Tim Federowicz referred him to Justin Turner's hitting instructor Doug Latta, and Williamson returned last spring with unmistakably Turner-ish movements in his swing. You know the ones: a lowered hand-set meant to increase the loft in his stroke and a more patient leg-lift to better store energy in his back hip. The effects came together on a cool April night at AT&T Park, when Williamson launched a mammoth, 464-foot blast to right-center, a head-turning homer that left fans wanting more. Alas, in addition to thumping another bomb, Williamson crashed head-first into a wall the next day, and concussion symptoms ruined the remainder of his season. Assuming he's healthy, Williamson will come to spring training out of options and with considerable intrigue still surrounding his new swing. That should secure his roster spot and give him a chance to shed the Quad-A tag for good.

YEAR	TEAM	LVL	AGE	PA	DRC+	VORP	BABIP	BRR	FRAA	WARP
2016	SAC	AAA	25	226	109	14.9	.306	0.5	LF(25): 1.8, RF(23): -1.0	0.4
2016	SFN	MLB	25	127	91	1.8	.268	0.0	RF(23): -0.9, LF(13): 2.2	0.3
2017	SAC	AAA	26	382	76	2.5	.301	1.8	RF(56): -2.0, LF(27): -2.5	-0.9
2017	SFN	MLB	26	73	67	3.3	.325	1.3	RF(12): -0.1, LF(9): -0.3	0.0
2018	SFN	MLB	27	105	80	1.6	.254	0.3	LF(25): -0.6, RF(2): -0.1	0.0
2018	SAC	AAA	27	215	118	14.8	.283	0.0	RF(31): -0.2, LF(13): 0.9	0.7
2019	SFN	MLB	28	338	82	4.1	.269	-0.4	LF -1, RF -1	0.0

Mac Williamson, continued

Batted Ball Distribution

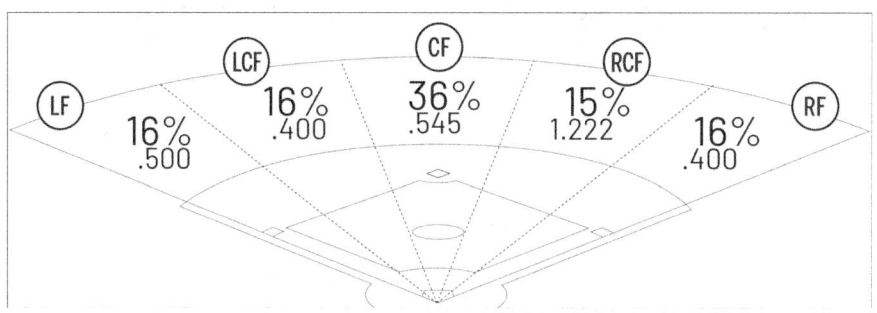

Strike Zone vs LHP

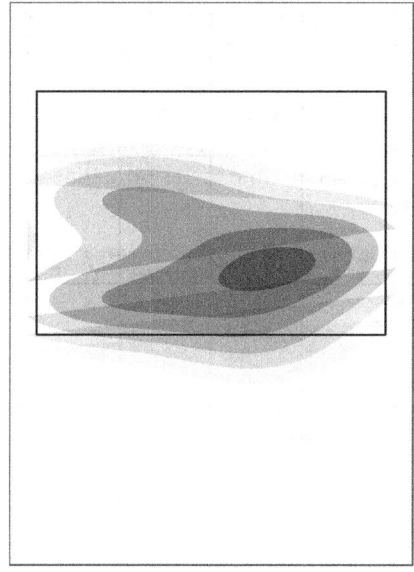

Strike Zone vs RHP

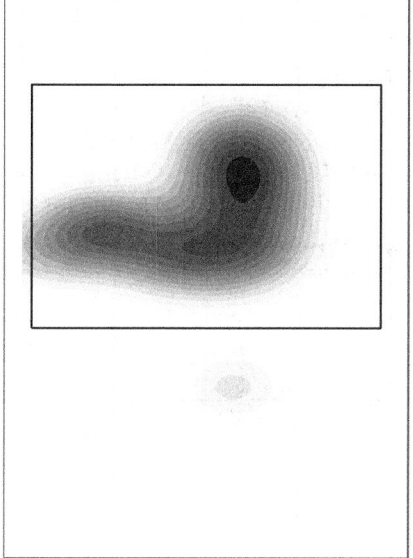

Ty Blach LHP

Born: 10/20/90 Age: 28 Bats: R Throws: L
Height: 6'1" Weight: 213 Origin: Round 5, 2012 Draft (#178 overall)

YEAR	TEAM	LVL	AGE	W	L	SV	G	GS	IP	H	HR	BB/9	K/9	K	GB%	BABIP
2016	SAC	AAA	25	14	7	0	26	26	162^2	147	9	2.1	6.3	113	50%	.280
2016	SFN	MLB	25	1	0	0	4	2	17	8	1	2.6	5.3	10	60%	.152
2017	SFN	MLB	26	8	12	0	34	24	163^2	179	17	2.4	4.0	73	48%	.290
2018	SFN	MLB	27	6	7	0	47	13	118^2	133	8	3.1	5.7	75	55%	.323
2019	SFN	MLB	28	4	5	0	40	8	73	75	7	3.0	6.0	49	50%	.294

Breakout: 7% Improve: 24% Collapse: 23% Attrition: 19% MLB: 63%
Comparables: Joe Biagini, Taylor Jordan, Jose Alvarez

"Utility man" applies exclusively to position players, but if there were an analogous job description for pitchers, Blach would fit that role to a T. He worked in almost every capacity in 2018, from starter to specialist, long guy to setup man, appearing at least once in every frame from the first through the 16th. Like a true utility man, Blach wasn't particularly adept at any job, but he was always up for the task at hand. And, since the little things set the best utility men apart, Blach made sure to field his position and hold runners, recording 24 assists without an error while holding foes to just three steals in six tries. Managers typically deploy utility men to keep their key regulars fresh, and the same usage best suits Blach. When a veteran starter needs an extra day, it's 10-to-nothing in the fifth inning or it's #weirdbaseball time in the 14th, Blach's there to do the job so his teammates don't have to.

YEAR	TEAM	LVL	AGE	WHIP	ERA	DRA	WARP	MPH	FB%	WHF	CSP
2016	SAC	AAA	25	1.14	3.43	4.08	2.4				
2016	SFN	MLB	25	0.76	1.06	5.57	-0.1	93.1	61.5	7.1	46.3
2017	SFN	MLB	26	1.36	4.78	4.75	1.5	91.5	60.1	7	50.5
2018	SFN	MLB	27	1.47	4.25	4.79	0.5	91.5	57.6	7.9	50.3
2019	SFN	MLB	28	1.35	4.19	4.64	0.3	91.0	59.3	7.5	49.7

Ty Blach, continued

Pitch Shape vs LHH

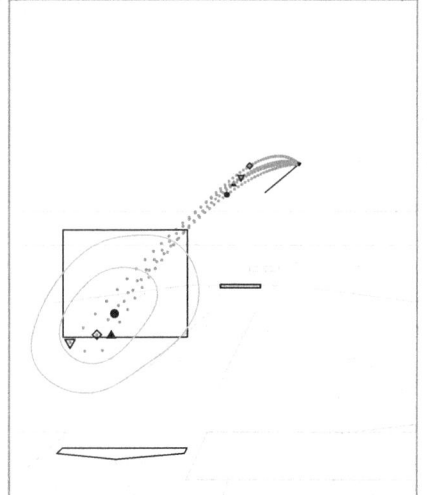

Pitch Shape vs RHH

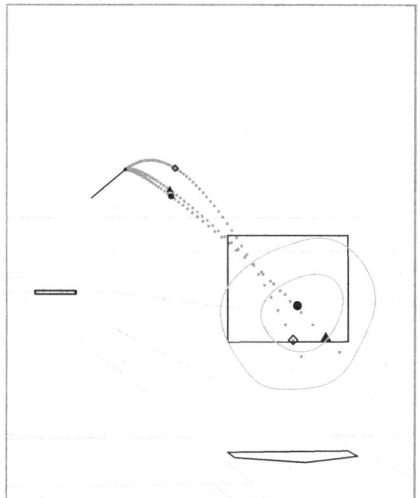

Type	Frequency	Velocity	H Movement	V Movement
● Fastball	57.6%	90.5 [94]	13.1 [70]	-20.5 [85]
☐ Sinker				
+ Cutter				
▲ Changeup	26.1%	80.3 [80]	15.7 [77]	-32.7 [84]
✕ Splitter				
▽ Slider	4.9%	79.3 [77]	-4.8 [100]	-40.9 [77]
◇ Curveball	11.4%	76.2 [92]	-6.8 [96]	-54 [86]
✥ Slow Curveball				
✱ Knuckleball				
▼ Screwball				

Ray Black RHP

Born: 06/26/90   Age: 29   Bats: R   Throws: R
Height: 6'5"   Weight: 225   Origin: Round 7, 2011 Draft (#237 overall)

YEAR	TEAM	LVL	AGE	W	L	SV	G	GS	IP	H	HR	BB/9	K/9	K	GB%	BABIP
2016	RIC	AA	26	1	4	6	35	0	31^1	17	1	9.2	15.2	53	39%	.286
2018	RIC	AA	28	0	0	4	10	0	10	4	0	3.6	18.0	20	7%	.286
2018	SAC	AAA	28	3	0	1	26	0	25^2	15	2	2.8	16.1	46	25%	.310
2018	SFN	MLB	28	2	2	0	26	0	23^1	17	4	3.9	12.7	33	41%	.277
2019	SFN	MLB	29	1	1	0	26	0	28	22	4	7.2	13.1	41	38%	.300

Breakout: 8%   Improve: 28%   Collapse: 21%   Attrition: 23%   MLB: 63%
Comparables: Ryan O'Rourke, Steve Delabar, James Hoyt

Tommy John surgery. A torn throwing-shoulder labrum. Bone spurs in the elbow. If there's an arm injury, Black's had it. From high school through his major-league debut at the age of 28, the right-hander tantalized scouts with a power fastball and devilish slider, and frequented surgeons with the medical consequences of throwing them. A seventh-round pick in 2011, he was the sort of prospect you rush to the majors as soon as his control passes muster, in hopes of extracting value before his arm gives in. But Black hit the disabled list with the aforementioned labrum tear in his very first Spring Training, and good control didn't coincide with good health until seven years later. He arrived with his arm scarred but still working, his fastball still electric, his slider still darting. The stuff will play in the late innings for as long as his arm is able to deliver it.

YEAR	TEAM	LVL	AGE	WHIP	ERA	DRA	WARP	MPH	FB%	WHF	CSP
2016	RIC	AA	26	1.56	4.88	1.61	1.2				
2018	RIC	AA	28	0.80	0.90	1.37	0.4				
2018	SAC	AAA	28	0.90	3.16	1.49	1.1				
2018	SFN	MLB	28	1.16	6.17	2.66	0.6	100.0	64	17.1	45.7
2019	SFN	MLB	29	1.59	4.83	5.04	-0.1	99.3	64	17.1	45.7

Ray Black, continued

Pitch Shape vs LHH

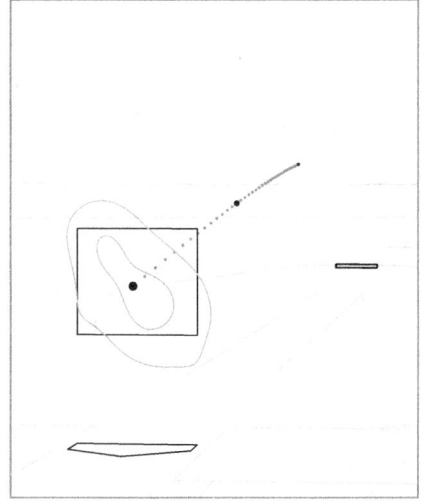

Pitch Shape vs RHH

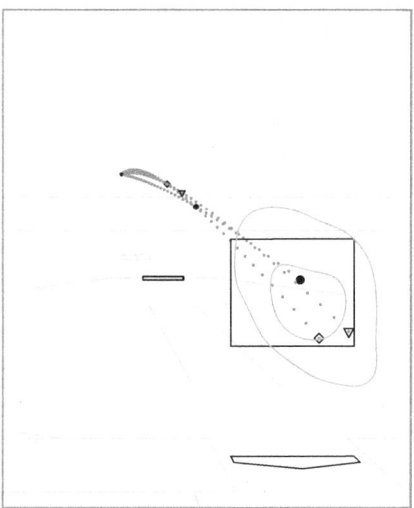

Type	Frequency	Velocity	H Movement	V Movement
● Fastball	64.0%	98.5 [119]	-4.7 [109]	-10.4 [117]
☐ Sinker				
+ Cutter				
▲ Changeup				
✕ Splitter				
▽ Slider	22.1%	86.2 [108]	11.6 [129]	-34.5 [96]
◇ Curveball	13.9%	82.4 [115]	13.6 [124]	-45 [107]
⊕ Slow Curveball				
✳ Knuckleball				
▼ Screwball				

San Francisco Giants 2019

Madison Bumgarner LHP
Born: 08/01/89 Age: 29 Bats: R Throws: L
Height: 6'4" Weight: 242 Origin: Round 1, 2007 Draft (#10 overall)

YEAR	TEAM	LVL	AGE	W	L	SV	G	GS	IP	H	HR	BB/9	K/9	K	GB%	BABIP
2016	SFN	MLB	26	15	9	0	34	34	226^2	179	26	2.1	10.0	251	41%	.267
2017	SJO	A+	27	0	1	0	2	2	10	11	4	1.8	11.7	13	29%	.292
2017	SFN	MLB	27	4	9	0	17	17	111	101	17	1.6	8.2	101	42%	.272
2018	SFN	MLB	28	6	7	0	21	21	129^2	118	14	3.0	7.6	109	43%	.274
2019	SFN	MLB	29	9	10	0	27	27	162	151	20	2.6	8.2	148	42%	.286

Breakout: 12%   Improve: 36%   Collapse: 18%   Attrition: 4%   MLB: 95%
Comparables: Masahiro Tanaka, David Price, Zack Greinke

When Bumgarner signed a long-term extension before the 2012 season, he secured the largest guarantee ever paid to a pitcher with less than two years of service time while delaying his free agency from 2018 to 2020. Had the left-hander hit the market after 2017, he would have been 28, still in the prime of his career, an ace whose sterling reputation was tainted only by poor judgment in riding a dirt bike. Instead, Bumgarner enters 2019 needing to shake his second straight freak-injury-shortened year, allay concerns about diminishing velocity and reestablish his standing as a frontline arm. A workhorse's workhorse, Bumgarner should flirt with 1,800 career innings before his 30th birthday, mileage that has taken a toll on his fastball. Opponents slugged .571 against his now-average four-seamer and struck out just 19 times in the 147 at-bats that ended with it. Bumgarner responded by throwing more curveballs and cutters, pitches that miss more bats but also miss the strike zone more often, yielding the highest walk rate of his career. Unless reversed, these trends threaten to cost a would-be $200 million pitcher half his earning potential. Among the top players in next winter's free agent class, Bumgarner may face the most pivotal contract year.

YEAR	TEAM	LVL	AGE	WHIP	ERA	DRA	WARP	MPH	FB%	WHF	CSP
2016	SFN	MLB	26	1.03	2.74	2.70	6.9	92.6	48.2	12.4	45.4
2017	SJO	A+	27	1.30	8.10	3.23	0.2				
2017	SFN	MLB	27	1.09	3.32	3.66	2.4	92.7	43	11.1	46
2018	SFN	MLB	28	1.24	3.26	4.47	1.3	91.9	34.4	10.1	49
2019	SFN	MLB	29	1.20	3.85	4.31	1.4	91.7	41.8	11.2	47.1

Madison Bumgarner, continued

Pitch Shape vs LHH

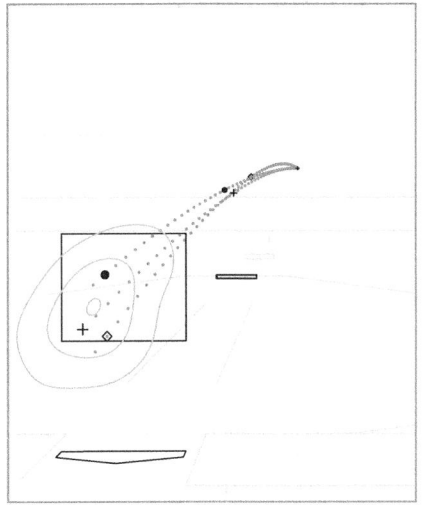

Pitch Shape vs RHH

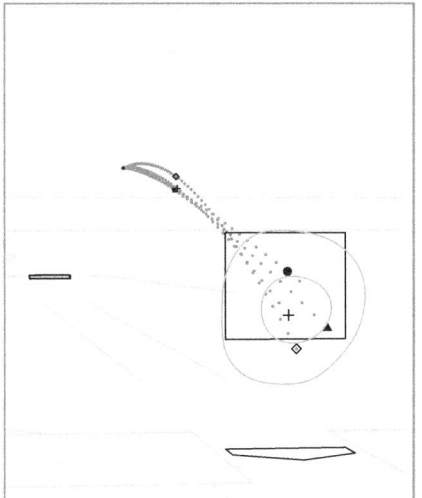

Type	Frequency	Velocity	H Movement	V Movement
● Fastball	34.4%	91.4 [96]	7.4 [97]	-17.4 [95]
☐ Sinker				
+ Cutter	35.2%	86 [83]	-2.3 [102]	-28.6 [80]
▲ Changeup	7.7%	84.1 [95]	11.9 [97]	-29.9 [92]
✕ Splitter				
▽ Slider				
◇ Curveball	22.2%	78.1 [99]	-7.5 [99]	-45.8 [105]
⊕ Slow Curveball	0.5%	71 [106]	-11.1 [101]	-55.2 [113]
✳ Knuckleball				
▼ Screwball				

Giants Player Analysis - 55

Johnny Cueto RHP

Born: 02/15/86 Age: 33 Bats: R Throws: R
Height: 5'11" Weight: 229 Origin: International Free Agent, 2004

YEAR	TEAM	LVL	AGE	W	L	SV	G	GS	IP	H	HR	BB/9	K/9	K	GB%	BABIP
2016	SFN	MLB	30	18	5	0	32	32	219^2	195	15	1.8	8.1	198	52%	.293
2017	SFN	MLB	31	8	8	0	25	25	147^1	160	22	3.2	8.3	136	41%	.322
2018	SFN	MLB	32	3	2	0	9	9	53	46	8	2.2	6.5	38	45%	.253
2019	SFN	MLB	33	1	1	0	3	3	15	14	2	2.6	7.7	13	45%	.293

Breakout: 13% Improve: 41% Collapse: 21% Attrition: 16% MLB: 96%
Comparables: Kelvim Escobar, Roy Oswalt, Cole Hamels

The opportunity to rehab an arm injury in lieu of surgery, to sit out two months instead of two years, is a glimmer of hope in a dark hour at the office of Dr. James Andrews. Coming off a five-start stretch of 0.84 ERA ball to start the season, Cueto took the rehab route, hopeful that if he could pitch so effectively through the soreness of a sprained UCL, it must not be so serious after all. Alas, the same pitcher who was nearly unhittable in April became a punching bag when he returned in July, and with his fastball scarcely touching 90 on the gun, Cueto gave in to Tommy John surgery that will sideline him until 2020. The right-hander will be 34 when he next shimmies and deals from a big-league rubber, amplifying the risk in a recovery that's not automatic even for pitchers 10 years younger. His guile and savvy should sustain him into the '20s, but his days as an ace have likely passed.

YEAR	TEAM	LVL	AGE	WHIP	ERA	DRA	WARP	MPH	FB%	WHF	CSP
2016	SFN	MLB	30	1.09	2.79	2.93	6.1	94.3	50.1	10.5	46.2
2017	SFN	MLB	31	1.45	4.52	4.57	1.7	93.2	51.2	11.4	42.7
2018	SFN	MLB	32	1.11	3.23	4.56	0.5	92.0	46.8	10	46.4
2019	SFN	MLB	33	1.21	3.95	4.41	0.1	92.4	49.4	10.6	44.6

Johnny Cueto, continued

Pitch Shape vs LHH

Pitch Shape vs RHH

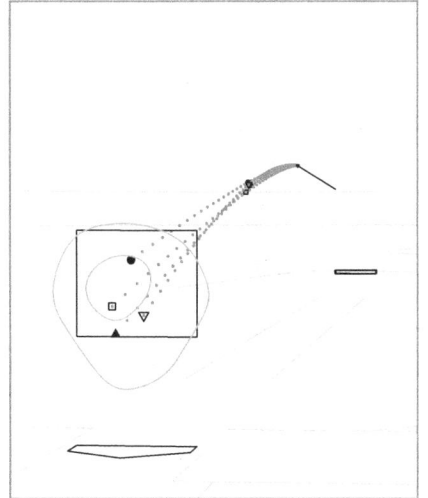
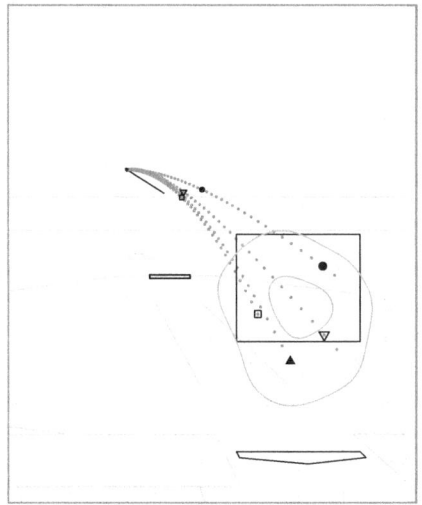

Type	Frequency	Velocity	H Movement	V Movement
● Fastball	26.5%	90.5 [94]	-7.7 [95]	-16.4 [98]
□ Sinker	20.3%	89.7 [86]	-13 [97]	-23 [91]
+ Cutter				
▲ Changeup	24.6%	82.3 [88]	-9.7 [109]	-33.8 [81]
× Splitter				
▽ Slider	26.0%	83.6 [96]	3 [92]	-31.1 [106]
◇ Curveball	2.6%	78.9 [101]	4.6 [86]	-41.6 [114]
⊕ Slow Curveball				
✳ Knuckleball				
▼ Screwball				

Sam Dyson RHP

Born: 05/07/88   Age: 31   Bats: R   Throws: R
Height: 6'1"   Weight: 212   Origin: Round 4, 2010 Draft (#126 overall)

YEAR	TEAM	LVL	AGE	W	L	SV	G	GS	IP	H	HR	BB/9	K/9	K	GB%	BABIP
2016	TEX	MLB	28	3	2	38	73	0	70^1	63	5	2.9	7.0	55	65%	.291
2017	TEX	MLB	29	1	6	0	17	0	16^2	31	6	6.5	3.8	7	62%	.379
2017	SFN	MLB	29	3	4	14	38	0	38	36	2	4.3	6.4	27	67%	.286
2018	SFN	MLB	30	4	3	3	74	0	70^1	56	5	2.6	7.2	56	62%	.270
2019	SFN	MLB	31	3	3	0	58	0	61	60	5	3.6	7.4	51	58%	.297

Breakout: 27%   Improve: 47%   Collapse: 24%   Attrition: 13%   MLB: 88%
Comparables: Chad Bradford, Eric O'Flaherty, John Franco

The importance of getting ahead in the count is one of baseball's few undisputed truths. In 2017, Dyson's first-pitch-strike rate plunged eight points to 53.1 percent, 17th-worst in the majors, and his opponents hit a Bonds-ian .364/.479/.636 after 1-0 counts. Having seen his career flash before his eyes, Dyson resolved to attack hitters with his best pitch, throwing his turbo sinker to start nearly three-fourths of the batters he faced. With renewed confidence in the heater, the right-hander restored his first-pitch-strike clip to its previous norm around 60 percent while retaining his place among the premier ground-ball generators in the league. A middling strikeout rate and trouble holding runners still make Dyson a dubious choice for saves, but he should be a quality middle-inning man as long as he can earn strike one.

YEAR	TEAM	LVL	AGE	WHIP	ERA	DRA	WARP	MPH	FB%	WHF	CSP
2016	TEX	MLB	28	1.22	2.43	4.48	0.4	98.2	70.5	8.7	49.9
2017	TEX	MLB	29	2.58	10.80	8.89	-0.7	96.6	73.8	6	47.2
2017	SFN	MLB	29	1.42	4.03	6.27	-0.5	96.7	73.8	10	48.3
2018	SFN	MLB	30	1.08	2.69	4.01	0.7	95.6	65.4	11.9	48.8
2019	SFN	MLB	31	1.37	4.02	4.44	0.3	95.7	69	10	48.5

Sam Dyson, continued

Pitch Shape vs LHH

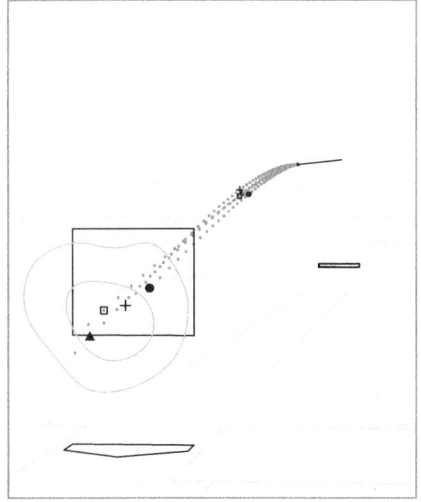

Pitch Shape vs RHH

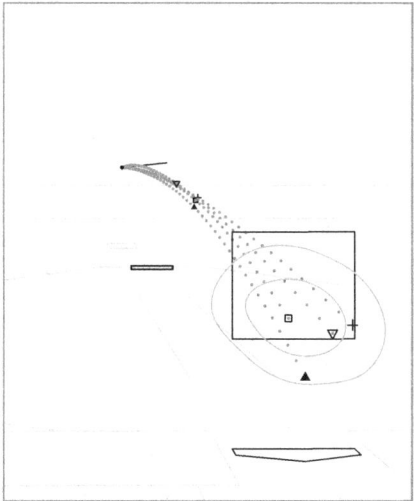

Type	Frequency	Velocity	H Movement	V Movement
● Fastball	7.0%	94.1 [105]	-5.4 [106]	-17.1 [96]
☐ Sinker	58.4%	94.1 [108]	-14.4 [85]	-24.2 [87]
+ Cutter	13.2%	89.8 [106]	2.7 [105]	-24.8 [96]
▲ Changeup	13.9%	87.3 [108]	-13.7 [87]	-31.4 [88]
× Splitter				
▽ Slider	7.5%	84.2 [99]	11.3 [128]	-38.5 [84]
◇ Curveball				
⊕ Slow Curveball				
✳ Knuckleball				
▼ Screwball				

San Francisco Giants 2019

Merandy Gonzalez   RHP
Born: 10/09/95   Age: 23   Bats: R   Throws: R
Height: 6'0"   Weight: 216   Origin: International Free Agent, 2013

YEAR	TEAM	LVL	AGE	W	L	SV	G	GS	IP	H	HR	BB/9	K/9	K	GB%	BABIP
2016	BRO	A-	20	6	3	0	14	14	69	65	2	3.5	9.3	71	54%	.337
2017	COL	A	21	8	1	0	11	11	69^2	50	3	1.7	8.4	65	43%	.253
2017	SLU	A+	21	4	2	0	6	6	36^1	33	1	2.0	5.9	24	43%	.271
2017	JUP	A+	21	1	0	1	5	3	24^1	18	0	1.8	5.2	14	56%	.247
2018	JAX	AA	22	3	6	0	14	14	73	68	7	4.1	5.8	47	41%	.282
2018	MIA	MLB	22	2	1	0	8	1	22	31	4	3.3	7.8	19	34%	.375
2019	SFN	MLB	23	4	6	1	23	14	84^1	86	13	4.0	7.1	67	40%	.305

Breakout: 3%   Improve: 8%   Collapse: 7%   Attrition: 9%   MLB: 18%
Comparables: Tom Gorzelanny, Yency Almonte, Trevor Oaks

It feels like the Marlins are hedging a bit with Gonzalez. Pegged by scouts to be a future reliever thanks to inconsistent fastball command and the lack of development on his changeup, the Fish insisted on keeping him as a starter. His strikeouts continued to wane and his walks doubled in his first taste of Double-A. Despite the mediocre results, the team surprisingly promoted him to the big-league bullpen in the early months, where he made seven appearances and struggled, though his strikeouts returned. His value to a major-league team remains in flux with his role questions, and he hasn't conquered either role recently.

YEAR	TEAM	LVL	AGE	WHIP	ERA	DRA	WARP	MPH	FB%	WHF	CSP
2016	BRO	A-	20	1.33	2.87	3.42	1.5				
2017	COL	A	21	0.90	1.55	3.10	1.8				
2017	SLU	A+	21	1.13	2.23	5.91	-0.3				
2017	JUP	A+	21	0.95	1.11	3.93	0.4				
2018	JAX	AA	22	1.38	4.32	4.92	0.4				
2018	MIA	MLB	22	1.77	5.73	7.39	-0.6	96.1	56.3	9.6	45.7
2019	SFN	MLB	23	1.47	5.10	5.91	-0.8	96.0	58.3	10	47.3

Merandy Gonzalez, continued

Pitch Shape vs LHH

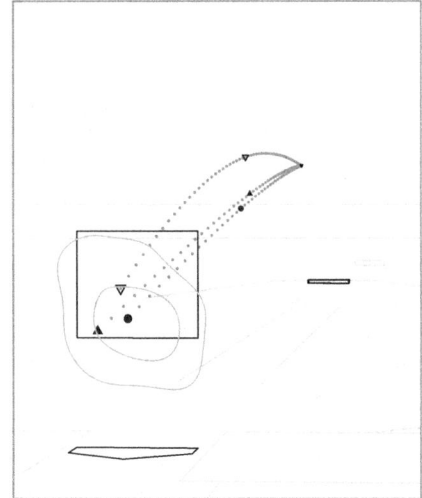

Pitch Shape vs RHH

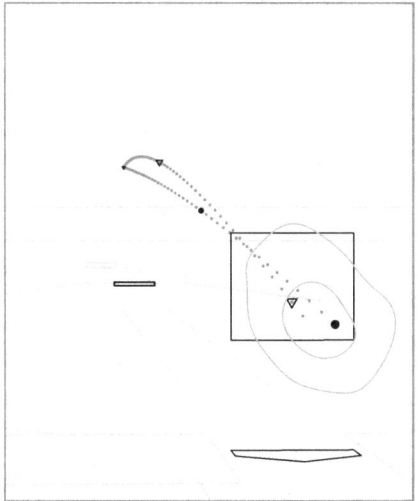

Type	Frequency	Velocity	H Movement	V Movement
● Fastball	56.3%	94 [105]	-2 [121]	-14.5 [104]
☐ Sinker				
+ Cutter				
▲ Changeup	10.1%	84.6 [97]	-10.5 [104]	-23.8 [111]
× Splitter				
▽ Slider	33.6%	76.5 [64]	11.9 [130]	-49.3 [52]
◇ Curveball				
⊕ Slow Curveball				
✷ Knuckleball				
▼ Screwball				

San Francisco Giants 2019

Derek Holland LHP

Born: 10/09/86   Age: 32   Bats: B   Throws: L
Height: 6'2"   Weight: 213   Origin: Round 25, 2006 Draft (#748 overall)

YEAR	TEAM	LVL	AGE	W	L	SV	G	GS	IP	H	HR	BB/9	K/9	K	GB%	BABIP
2016	ROU	AAA	29	0	0	0	3	3	10	11	1	3.6	7.2	8	58%	.312
2016	TEX	MLB	29	7	9	0	22	20	107^1	116	15	2.9	5.6	67	38%	.295
2017	CHA	MLB	30	7	14	0	29	26	135	156	31	5.0	6.9	104	39%	.307
2018	SFN	MLB	31	7	9	0	36	30	171^1	154	19	3.5	8.9	169	42%	.288
2019	SFN	MLB	32	7	9	0	37	21	128	122	16	3.5	8.5	121	40%	.294

Breakout: 28%   Improve: 53%   Collapse: 17%   Attrition: 11%   MLB: 86%
Comparables: Edwin Jackson, Claudio Vargas, Bud Norris

In 2017, Holland was the very worst pitcher in baseball, below replacement level by any value metric and buried deep beneath it by DRA. With his career hanging by a thread, the lefty chose San Francisco for his revival, betting on himself to win a roster spot, and on the cushy ballpark and savvy coaching staff to perform CPR. Injuries afforded Holland the opportunity he sought, and after just gobbling innings for two months and change, he turned a corner with two midseason adjustments. After working from the third-base edge of the rubber through June 15th, Holland shifted to the first-base side, giving hitters a sharper angle. At the same time, he swapped many of his curveballs for sliders, and the change in his positioning gave the breaking ball more room to work back toward the plate. By year's end, Holland boasted a career-high whiff rate while throwing his highest share of pitches in the zone since 2012. Those improvements came at a price—right-handed foes posted a .798 OPS to lefties' .440—but on balance, he was much better for them. Back on the right side of the replacement-level bar, Holland should have value in a swing role again this year.

YEAR	TEAM	LVL	AGE	WHIP	ERA	DRA	WARP	MPH	FB%	WHF	CSP
2016	ROU	AAA	29	1.50	4.50	3.83	0.2				
2016	TEX	MLB	29	1.41	4.95	6.48	-1.4	94.5	61.4	8.3	46.7
2017	CHA	MLB	30	1.71	6.20	8.59	-4.6	93.1	55.1	7.8	45.1
2018	SFN	MLB	31	1.29	3.57	3.80	2.9	93.3	56.9	11.2	49.5
2019	SFN	MLB	32	1.35	4.18	4.65	0.6	92.5	56.6	9.4	46.9

Derek Holland, continued

Pitch Shape vs LHH

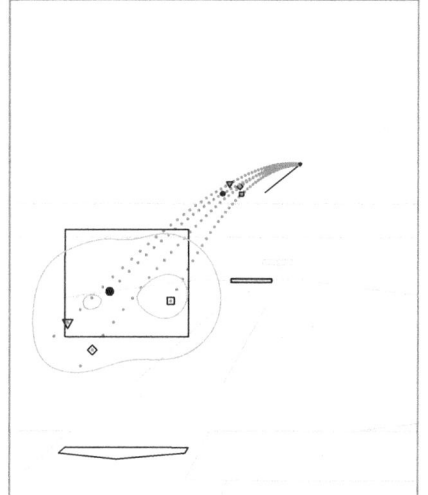

Pitch Shape vs RHH

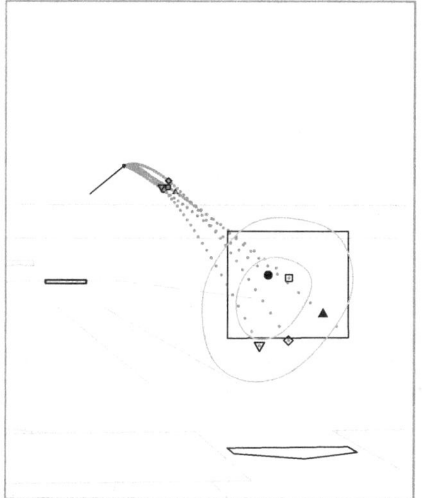

Type	Frequency	Velocity	H Movement	V Movement
● Fastball	34.8%	92.2 [99]	12.5 [73]	-15.7 [100]
☐ Sinker	22.1%	92 [98]	15.3 [77]	-19.6 [103]
+ Cutter				
▲ Changeup	8.3%	83.5 [93]	11.2 [100]	-22.2 [115]
× Splitter				
▽ Slider	20.3%	81 [85]	1.3 [73]	-34 [97]
◇ Curveball	14.5%	79.8 [105]	0.4 [65]	-37.4 [124]
⊕ Slow Curveball				
✳ Knuckleball				
▼ Screwball				

San Francisco Giants 2019

Mark Melancon   RHP
Born: 03/28/85   Age: 34   Bats: R   Throws: R
Height: 6'2"   Weight: 215   Origin: Round 9, 2006 Draft (#284 overall)

YEAR	TEAM	LVL	AGE	W	L	SV	G	GS	IP	H	HR	BB/9	K/9	K	GB%	BABIP
2016	PIT	MLB	31	1	1	30	45	0	41²	31	2	1.9	8.2	38	49%	.257
2016	WAS	MLB	31	1	1	17	30	0	29²	21	1	0.9	8.2	27	65%	.263
2017	SFN	MLB	32	1	2	11	32	0	30	37	3	1.8	8.7	29	54%	.374
2018	SFN	MLB	33	1	4	3	41	0	39	48	2	3.2	7.2	31	52%	.365
2019	SFN	MLB	34	2	2	6	48	0	50	50	6	3.1	7.3	41	50%	.294

Breakout: 14%   Improve: 35%   Collapse: 34%   Attrition: 7%   MLB: 89%
Comparables: Mariano Rivera, Heath Bell, Bob Howry

The Giants have a long list of real good reasons for all the things they've done—even briefly making Melancon the highest-paid reliever (by average annual value) in baseball history. You could cry for the money they've wasted, but that's a waste of time and tears. So instead of dwelling on the $62 million lost, note that Melancon—dogged by forearm woes in his first two seasons out west—ended 2018 with a healthy right arm. Note, also, his velocity climbed over the year, more than half the balls in play against him were on the ground and the advanced metrics saw an above-average pitcher, albeit not a dominant one. If you cast the financial baggage aside, you'll find that Melancon enters 2019 as a decent seventh-inning arm, and you do need those. So forgive everything that forgiveness will allow; there's nothing you or the Giants can do about it now.

YEAR	TEAM	LVL	AGE	WHIP	ERA	DRA	WARP	MPH	FB%	WHF	CSP
2016	PIT	MLB	31	0.96	1.51	2.64	1.1	93.3	73.3	11	43.7
2016	WAS	MLB	31	0.81	1.82	2.47	0.9	93.7	73.3	12.3	44.9
2017	SFN	MLB	32	1.43	4.50	2.75	0.8	93.1	74.7	10.6	43.9
2018	SFN	MLB	33	1.59	3.23	3.62	0.6	92.9	68.3	10.6	46.2
2019	SFN	MLB	34	1.33	4.21	4.60	0.1	92.1	70.6	10.8	44.3

Mark Melancon, continued

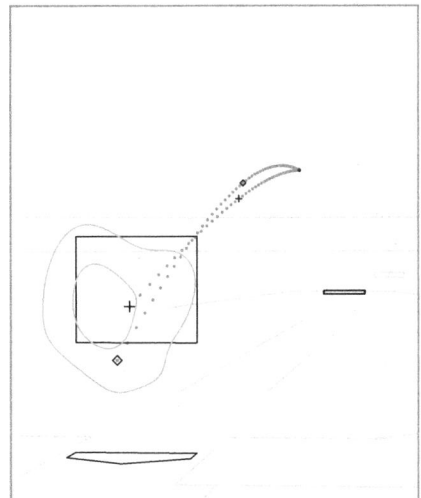

Pitch Shape vs LHH

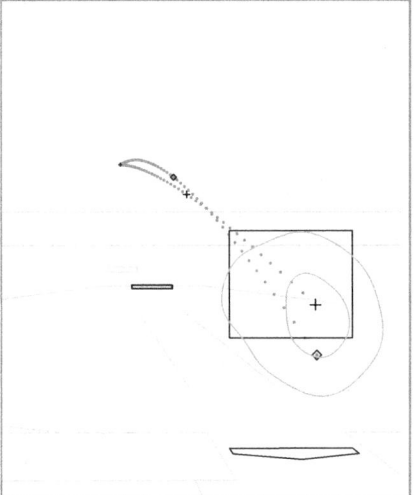

Pitch Shape vs RHH

Type	Frequency	Velocity	H Movement	V Movement
● Fastball	7.4%	92 [98]	-5.6 [105]	-18.6 [91]
☐ Sinker				
+ Cutter	60.9%	91.8 [118]	1.7 [99]	-21.2 [110]
▲ Changeup				
× Splitter	3.4%	82.8 [84]	-9.5 [95]	-27.1 [110]
▽ Slider				
◇ Curveball	28.4%	83.2 [117]	4.2 [85]	-47.7 [101]
⊕ Slow Curveball				
✻ Knuckleball				
▼ Screwball				

San Francisco Giants 2019

Reyes Moronta   RHP
Born: 01/06/93   Age: 26   Bats: R   Throws: R
Height: 5'11"   Weight: 241   Origin: International Free Agent, 2011

YEAR	TEAM	LVL	AGE	W	L	SV	G	GS	IP	H	HR	BB/9	K/9	K	GB%	BABIP
2016	SJO	A+	23	0	3	14	60	0	59	43	7	3.1	14.2	93	34%	.295
2017	RIC	AA	24	0	1	5	19	0	18	15	1	6.0	13.0	26	42%	.333
2017	SAC	AAA	24	3	0	0	13	0	17	13	1	4.2	9.0	17	33%	.273
2017	SFN	MLB	24	0	0	0	7	0	6^2	6	1	4.1	14.9	11	47%	.357
2018	SFN	MLB	25	5	2	1	69	0	65	34	4	5.1	10.9	79	43%	.211
2019	SFN	MLB	26	3	3	0	53	0	56	47	6	4.9	11.1	69	39%	.298

Breakout: 19%   Improve: 35%   Collapse: 26%   Attrition: 27%   MLB: 75%
Comparables: Enrique Burgos, Tommy Kahnle, Bruce Rondon

If there were a GIF dictionary for scouting terms, you'd find one of Moronta pitching under the listing for "max-effort delivery." The short, squat right-hander kicks his leg high, whirls back, loads his right arm deep and throws his weight around in a ferocious uncoiling of his body that sends electric stuff in the general direction of home plate. When his high-90s heaters cross over the white, setting up Moronta's hard diving slider, the tandem rivals those of the game's top closers. But with Moronta's strenuous motion and below-average athleticism come the sort of control woes that would bind fans and managers together in fear if they arose in the ninth. Moronta tunnels his fastball and slider well, racking up whiffs with both, but his inability to massage the breaker in for looking strikes frequently leaves him behind in the count. Already a weapon in middle-inning jams, the Dominican is a few more sliders in the zone from joining the most feared late-game arms in the league.

YEAR	TEAM	LVL	AGE	WHIP	ERA	DRA	WARP	MPH	FB%	WHF	CSP
2016	SJO	A+	23	1.07	2.59	2.03	2.1				
2017	RIC	AA	24	1.50	4.00	2.63	0.5				
2017	SAC	AAA	24	1.24	2.12	4.04	0.2				
2017	SFN	MLB	24	1.35	2.70	2.60	0.2	97.5	52.7	16.4	50.2
2018	SFN	MLB	25	1.09	2.49	3.09	1.4	98.4	51	14.8	47.2
2019	SFN	MLB	26	1.38	3.79	4.24	0.4	97.9	52	15.2	49.4

Reyes Moronta, continued

Pitch Shape vs LHH

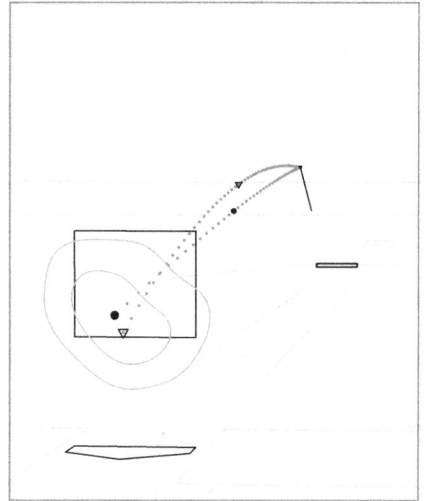

Pitch Shape vs RHH

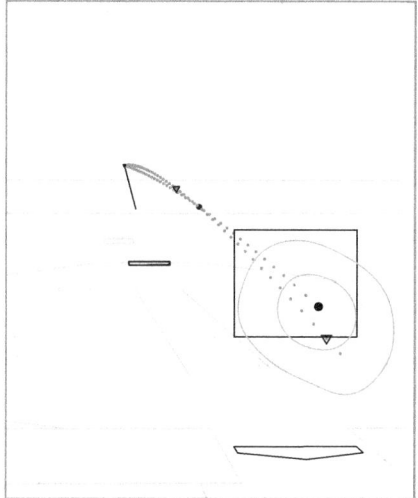

Type	Frequency	Velocity	H Movement	V Movement
● Fastball	51.0%	97.5 [116]	-2.5 [119]	-11.8 [112]
☐ Sinker				
+ Cutter				
▲ Changeup	0.2%	87.6 [109]	-8.6 [114]	-21.4 [117]
× Splitter				
▽ Slider	48.5%	83 [93]	11.7 [130]	-34.8 [95]
◇ Curveball	0.4%	79.9 [105]	11.1 [114]	-37.6 [124]
⊕ Slow Curveball				
✳ Knuckleball				
▼ Screwball				

San Francisco Giants 2019

Drew Pomeranz LHP

Born: 11/22/88 Age: 30 Bats: R Throws: L
Height: 6'6" Weight: 240 Origin: Round 1, 2010 Draft (#5 overall)

YEAR	TEAM	LVL	AGE	W	L	SV	G	GS	IP	H	HR	BB/9	K/9	K	GB%	BABIP
2016	SDN	MLB	27	8	7	0	17	17	102	67	8	3.6	10.1	115	50%	.240
2016	BOS	MLB	27	3	5	0	14	13	68[2]	70	14	3.1	9.3	71	47%	.306
2017	BOS	MLB	28	17	6	0	32	32	173[2]	166	19	3.6	9.0	174	45%	.310
2018	PAW	AAA	29	0	2	0	5	5	19[2]	16	7	5.9	5.5	12	58%	.173
2018	BOS	MLB	29	2	6	0	26	11	74	87	12	5.4	8.0	66	39%	.344
2019	SFN	MLB	30	6	7	0	29	18	106	99	12	3.7	7.9	93	44%	.288

Breakout: 9% Improve: 43% Collapse: 30% Attrition: 11% MLB: 90%
Comparables: David Phelps, Jon Lester, Lance Lynn

Last year's *Annual* comment noted that Pomeranz would be in for a big payday if he could just stay healthy in 2018. RON HOWARD VOICE: He couldn't. The artist formerly known as "Big Smooth" started the year on the DL with a left forearm flexor strain and ended up back on the DL in June with a combo biceps/neck issue. When he did manage to take the mound, Pomeranz was so ineffective that he finished last—yes, last—in the majors in DRA among pitchers with at least 70 IP. The Sox moved Pomeranz to the bullpen in early August in the hopes he'd at least emerge as a lefty matchup option. RON HOWARD VOICE: He didn't. Pomeranz allowed a .300/.394/.461 line as a reliever en route to getting left off two straight postseason rosters before quizzically making the cut for the World Series, where he was the only player on either roster who didn't appear in any games, 18-inning or otherwise. Instead of a lucrative multi-year deal, expect Pomeranz to settle for a pillow contract this offseason as he looks to rebuild some value.

YEAR	TEAM	LVL	AGE	WHIP	ERA	DRA	WARP	MPH	FB%	WHF	CSP
2016	SDN	MLB	27	1.06	2.47	3.08	2.7	93.5	58.4	12	44.7
2016	BOS	MLB	27	1.37	4.59	3.82	1.2	94.0	58.4	11.5	46.6
2017	BOS	MLB	28	1.35	3.32	4.17	2.7	93.5	61.6	10.6	43.1
2018	PAW	AAA	29	1.47	5.49	4.17	0.3				
2018	BOS	MLB	29	1.77	6.08	7.90	-2.3	91.6	58.9	7.9	43.7
2019	SFN	MLB	30	1.34	4.21	4.68	0.4	92.4	59.7	10.3	43.8

Drew Pomeranz, continued

Pitch Shape vs LHH

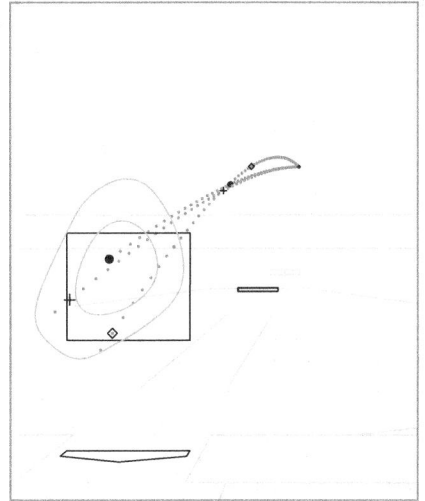

Pitch Shape vs RHH

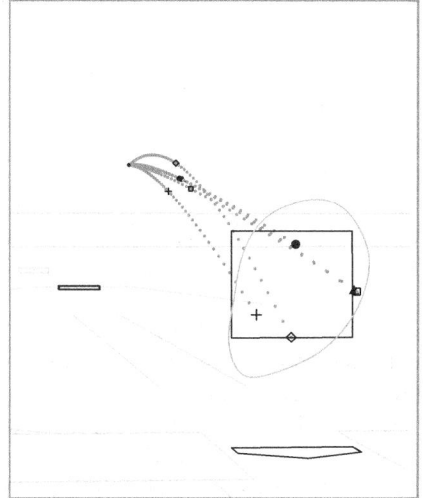

Type	Frequency	Velocity	H Movement	V Movement
● Fastball	39.4%	89.8 [91]	6.1 [103]	-14.9 [103]
□ Sinker	12.2%	88.7 [81]	12.9 [98]	-18.8 [105]
+ Cutter	7.3%	86.1 [84]	0.6 [85]	-23.1 [103]
▲ Changeup	2.1%	83 [91]	13.1 [90]	-24.4 [109]
× Splitter				
▽ Slider				
◇ Curveball	39.0%	78.3 [100]	-4.8 [87]	-54.7 [85]
✦ Slow Curveball				
✳ Knuckleball				
▼ Screwball				

Dereck Rodriguez RHP

Born: 06/05/92 Age: 27 Bats: R Throws: R
Height: 6'1" Weight: 215 Origin: Round 6, 2011 Draft (#208 overall)

YEAR	TEAM	LVL	AGE	W	L	SV	G	GS	IP	H	HR	BB/9	K/9	K	GB%	BABIP
2016	CDR	A	24	4	11	0	18	18	101	98	7	3.4	8.3	93	41%	.311
2016	FTM	A+	24	1	2	0	5	5	31²	29	4	0.6	5.1	18	41%	.250
2017	FTM	A+	25	5	2	0	11	11	68	59	7	1.5	7.8	59	43%	.278
2017	CHT	AA	25	5	4	0	15	13	75¹	74	9	3.2	7.4	62	41%	.294
2018	SAC	AAA	26	4	1	0	9	9	50¹	49	11	2.0	9.5	53	39%	.284
2018	SFN	MLB	26	6	4	0	21	19	118¹	98	9	2.7	6.8	89	41%	.257
2019	SFN	MLB	27	6	9	0	21	21	119²	119	19	3.0	7.7	102	39%	.288

Breakout: 13% Improve: 21% Collapse: 22% Attrition: 33% MLB: 64%
Comparables: Tyler Wilson, Kyle Lobstein, Albert Suarez

While the outgoing Giants regime fell short in many areas of roster building, its enduring strength was mining gems in minor-league free agency, where they found Rodriguez last winter. A converted outfielder who moved to the mound with the Twins only in 2014, the right-hander was Bobby Evans' parting gift to Farhan Zaidi, who inherited at least a durable back-end starter and potentially much more. Armed with Hall of Fame bloodlines, a sturdy lower half and four pitches he could throw for strikes, Pudge's son defied middling peripherals to rank 10th in ERA among pitchers with at least as many innings. Caution flags—from a .257 BABIP to a 6.9 percent HR/FB rate—abound in his rookie campaign, but so did causes for optimism; his inexperience and low mileage leave ample room for growth on the bump. With gobs of problems to solve and limited financial resources at his disposal, Zaidi will be happy to have a controllable mid-rotation arm in Rodriguez.

YEAR	TEAM	LVL	AGE	WHIP	ERA	DRA	WARP	MPH	FB%	WHF	CSP
2016	CDR	A	24	1.35	5.08	3.61	1.7				
2016	FTM	A+	24	0.98	2.56	3.81	0.6				
2017	FTM	A+	25	1.03	2.51	3.89	1.1				
2017	CHT	AA	25	1.34	3.94	3.88	1.1				
2018	SAC	AAA	26	1.19	3.40	4.31	0.7				
2018	SFN	MLB	26	1.13	2.81	5.18	0.1	94.3	53.3	9.9	48
2019	SFN	MLB	27	1.31	4.63	5.16	-0.1	93.8	53.9	10.1	48.6

Dereck Rodriguez, continued

Pitch Shape vs LHH

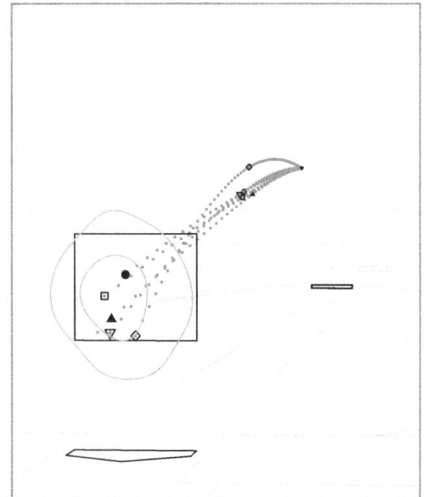

Pitch Shape vs RHH

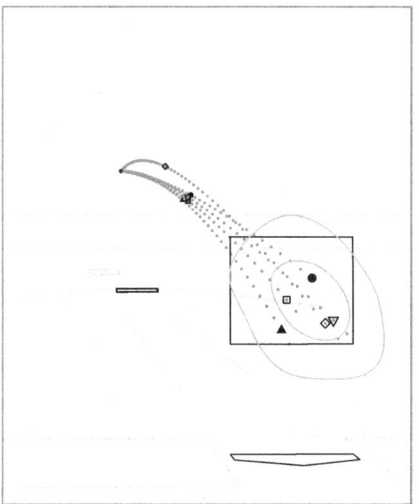

Type	Frequency	Velocity	H Movement	V Movement
● Fastball	37.1%	92.1 [99]	-3.4 [115]	-14.8 [103]
□ Sinker	16.2%	91.3 [94]	-10.4 [118]	-17.4 [110]
+ Cutter				
▲ Changeup	16.5%	84.9 [98]	-12.9 [91]	-25.1 [107]
× Splitter				
▽ Slider	11.4%	86.4 [109]	3.4 [94]	-26.5 [119]
◇ Curveball	18.8%	75.9 [91]	11.7 [116]	-53 [89]
⊕ Slow Curveball				
✳ Knuckleball				
▼ Screwball				

Jeff Samardzija RHP

Born: 01/23/85 Age: 34 Bats: R Throws: R
Height: 6'5" Weight: 240 Origin: Round 5, 2006 Draft (#149 overall)

YEAR	TEAM	LVL	AGE	W	L	SV	G	GS	IP	H	HR	BB/9	K/9	K	GB%	BABIP
2016	SFN	MLB	31	12	11	0	32	32	203^1	190	24	2.4	7.4	167	47%	.285
2017	SFN	MLB	32	9	15	0	32	32	207^2	204	30	1.4	8.9	205	43%	.303
2018	SAC	AAA	33	0	2	0	4	4	17	17	5	1.6	10.6	20	40%	.286
2018	SFN	MLB	33	1	5	0	10	10	44^2	47	6	5.2	6.0	30	32%	.287
2019	SFN	MLB	34	7	10	0	24	24	136	135	19	2.9	7.6	116	41%	.291

Breakout: 17% Improve: 39% Collapse: 15% Attrition: 4% MLB: 85%
Comparables: Ben Sheets, Jake Peavy, Hisashi Iwakuma

After leading the National League in innings in 2017, Samardzija ceded his reputation for durability to shoulder inflammation that wouldn't subside. The right-hander made three separate trips to the disabled list, had pain-killing injections and tried various rehab protocols, none of which got the workhorse's arm in working order. His 10 starts came in three separate spurts, all marred by a diminished fastball and trouble getting loose. The same pitcher who struck out nearly 6.5 batters for every walk in 2017 could barely keep the ratio above water a year later. On the bright side, doctors agreed that surgery was unnecessary and rest would eventually get Samardzija ready to pitch again. Assuming that happens, he'll be a fine innings-chewer, the sort of mid-rotation starter who can keep the relievers fresh for bullpenning when the no. 5 spot in the rotation comes around.

YEAR	TEAM	LVL	AGE	WHIP	ERA	DRA	WARP	MPH	FB%	WHF	CSP
2016	SFN	MLB	31	1.20	3.81	3.44	4.5	96.7	67.3	10	49.5
2017	SFN	MLB	32	1.14	4.42	3.43	5.0	96.3	56.8	11.1	50.5
2018	SAC	AAA	33	1.18	5.29	3.86	0.3				
2018	SFN	MLB	33	1.63	6.25	7.20	-1.0	95.1	63.2	9.2	46.3
2019	SFN	MLB	34	1.30	4.33	4.84	0.3	95.1	60.6	10.3	47.8

Jeff Samardzija, continued

Pitch Shape vs LHH

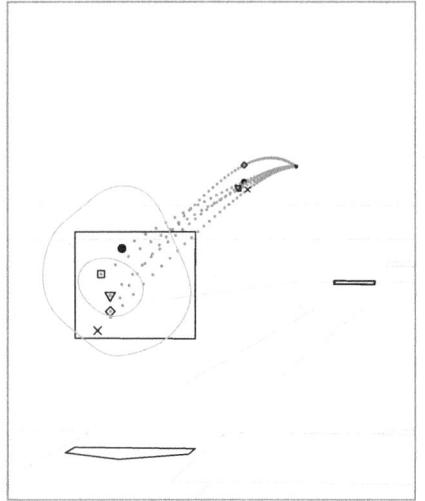

Pitch Shape vs RHH

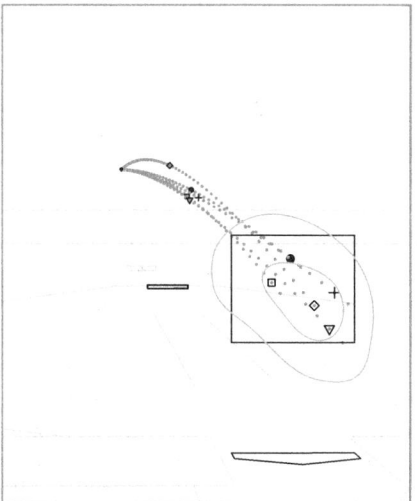

Type		Frequency	Velocity	H Movement	V Movement
●	Fastball	12.7%	93.1 [102]	-9 [89]	-14.3 [105]
□	Sinker	41.6%	93 [103]	-12.4 [102]	-16.5 [113]
+	Cutter	8.9%	91 [113]	-3.5 [69]	-17.4 [125]
▲	Changeup	0.2%	82.8 [90]	-10 [107]	-27.2 [100]
×	Splitter	6.1%	83.2 [87]	-10.4 [91]	-27.1 [110]
▽	Slider	19.4%	87.1 [112]	-1.4 [73]	-24 [127]
◇	Curveball	11.1%	77.3 [96]	3 [80]	-47.1 [102]
⊕	Slow Curveball				
✳	Knuckleball				
▼	Screwball				

San Francisco Giants 2019

Will Smith LHP
Born: 07/10/89   Age: 29   Bats: R   Throws: L
Height: 6'5"   Weight: 248   Origin: Round 7, 2008 Draft (#229 overall)

YEAR	TEAM	LVL	AGE	W	L	SV	G	GS	IP	H	HR	BB/9	K/9	K	GB%	BABIP
2016	MIL	MLB	26	1	3	0	27	0	22	18	3	3.7	9.0	22	42%	.263
2016	SFN	MLB	26	1	1	0	26	0	18[1]	13	0	4.4	12.8	26	40%	.325
2018	SFN	MLB	28	2	3	14	54	0	53	37	3	2.5	12.1	71	41%	.281
2019	SFN	MLB	29	3	3	24	53	0	56	48	6	3.9	10.8	67	41%	.302

Breakout: 20%   Improve: 49%   Collapse: 37%   Attrition: 10%   MLB: 97%
Comparables: Francisco Rodriguez, Antonio Bastardo, Jonathan Broxto

If you didn't get Smith on the first or second pitch of your at-bat last season, chances are, you were doomed. His foes hit .378 and slugged .600 on 0-0, 1-0 and 0-1 counts; those who waited longer hit .137 and slugged .185. The ex-Brewer returned from Tommy John surgery with a bulldog mindset and an unhittable slider, the former getting him ahead, the latter putting opponents away. Promoted to closer at the end of June, he thrived in high-leverage spots, trailing only Josh Hader, Aroldis Chapman and Brad Hand in strikeout rate among southpaw relievers with at least 50 innings. A free agent after the 2019 season, Smith is poised to be the market's most coveted bullpen lefty if he repeats that body of work.

YEAR	TEAM	LVL	AGE	WHIP	ERA	DRA	WARP	MPH	FB%	WHF	CSP
2016	MIL	MLB	26	1.23	3.68	4.57	0.1	94.2	55.4	9.7	45.5
2016	SFN	MLB	26	1.20	2.95	2.20	0.6	95.0	43.9	14.7	42.1
2018	SFN	MLB	28	0.98	2.55	3.34	1.0	94.4	46.1	15.8	50.7
2019	SFN	MLB	29	1.30	3.20	3.74	0.7	93.8	47.4	14.6	48.1

Will Smith, continued

Pitch Shape vs LHH

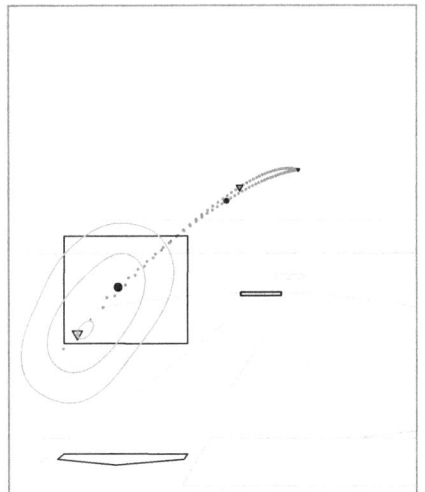

Pitch Shape vs RHH

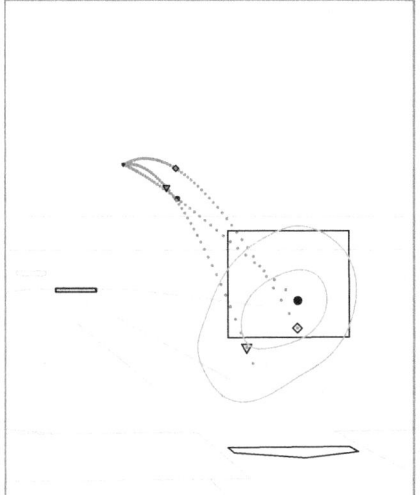

Type	Frequency	Velocity	H Movement	V Movement
● Fastball	46.1%	93.1 [102]	6.9 [99]	-13.7 [107]
☐ Sinker				
+ Cutter				
▲ Changeup	1.1%	87.7 [109]	12.2 [95]	-21.8 [116]
✕ Splitter				
▽ Slider	36.5%	81.6 [87]	-7.8 [113]	-36.2 [91]
◇ Curveball	16.3%	77.9 [98]	-7.1 [97]	-45.6 [106]
⊕ Slow Curveball				
✳ Knuckleball				
▼ Screwball				

San Francisco Giants 2019

Chris Stratton RHP

Born: 08/22/90 Age: 28 Bats: R Throws: R
Height: 6'2" Weight: 211 Origin: Round 1, 2012 Draft (#20 overall)

YEAR	TEAM	LVL	AGE	W	L	SV	G	GS	IP	H	HR	BB/9	K/9	K	GB%	BABIP
2016	SFN	MLB	25	1	0	0	7	0	10	11	1	4.5	5.4	6	38%	.323
2016	SAC	AAA	25	12	6	0	21	20	125^2	120	6	2.8	7.4	103	45%	.305
2017	SAC	AAA	26	4	5	0	15	15	79^1	94	10	2.5	8.1	71	53%	.340
2017	SFN	MLB	26	4	4	1	13	10	58^2	59	5	4.3	7.8	51	46%	.316
2018	SAC	AAA	27	3	0	0	4	4	24	25	3	3.0	9.0	24	44%	.324
2018	SFN	MLB	27	10	10	0	28	26	145	153	19	3.4	7.0	112	44%	.306
2019	SFN	MLB	28	5	6	0	43	11	91	94	12	3.3	7.4	76	44%	.298

Breakout: 17% Improve: 38% Collapse: 14% Attrition: 26% MLB: 69%
Comparables: Tanner Roark, Darrell Rasner, Cha Seung Baek

Complete-game shutouts are a dying breed in the era of bullpenning, but 20 pitchers earned their managers' trust to record 27 outs last season. The list was a who's who of Cy Young contenders and breakout flamethrowers, plus a few randos like Stratton, who two-hit the Rockies in the midst of their September surge. One of the league's leaders in curveball spin rate for two years running, the right-hander is oddly reluctant to lean on the hook, placing his faith in a fringy fastball that requires pinpoint command. When he has it, he can silence a powerful lineup. When he doesn't, he's just a serviceable fifth starter, another endangered species that openers and multi-inning relievers might soon supplant for good.

YEAR	TEAM	LVL	AGE	WHIP	ERA	DRA	WARP	MPH	FB%	WHF	CSP
2016	SFN	MLB	25	1.60	3.60	5.01	0.0	94.1	61.7	8.4	45.2
2016	SAC	AAA	25	1.27	3.87	3.38	2.8				
2017	SAC	AAA	26	1.46	5.11	3.86	1.6				
2017	SFN	MLB	26	1.48	3.68	4.62	0.6	93.3	62.4	9.9	45.5
2018	SAC	AAA	27	1.38	3.00	3.83	0.5				
2018	SFN	MLB	27	1.43	5.09	4.99	0.5	92.6	62.2	9.6	49.9
2019	SFN	MLB	28	1.39	4.41	4.83	0.1	92.3	62.6	9.7	47.5

Chris Stratton, continued

Pitch Shape vs LHH

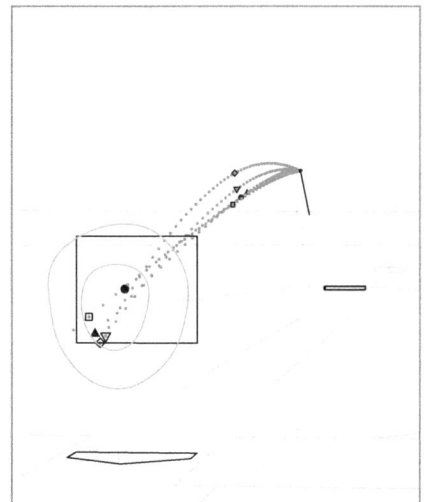

Pitch Shape vs RHH

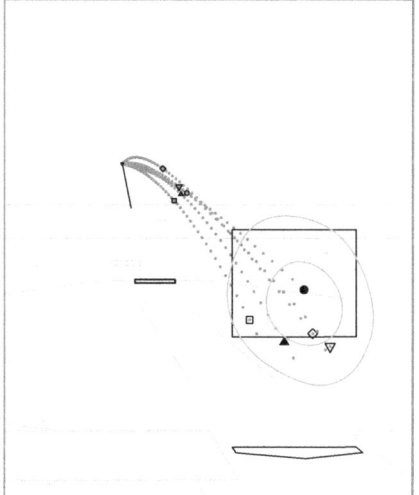

Type	Frequency	Velocity	H Movement	V Movement
● Fastball	56.2%	91.7 [97]	-2.5 [119]	-16.2 [99]
□ Sinker	6.0%	91.2 [94]	-8.8 [132]	-20 [101]
+ Cutter				
▲ Changeup	10.1%	84.6 [97]	-9.9 [107]	-29.7 [93]
× Splitter				
▽ Slider	12.7%	84 [98]	5.3 [102]	-35.8 [92]
◇ Curveball	15.0%	78.3 [99]	14.4 [127]	-50.5 [94]
⊕ Slow Curveball				
✳ Knuckleball				
▼ Screwball				

Andrew Suarez   LHP

Born: 09/11/92   Age: 26   Bats: L   Throws: L
Height: 6'0"   Weight: 187   Origin: Round 2, 2015 Draft (#61 overall)

YEAR	TEAM	LVL	AGE	W	L	SV	G	GS	IP	H	HR	BB/9	K/9	K	GB%	BABIP
2016	SJO	A+	23	2	1	0	5	5	29^2	25	2	1.5	10.3	34	61%	.299
2016	RIC	AA	23	7	7	0	19	19	114	129	11	1.9	7.1	90	48%	.332
2017	RIC	AA	24	4	4	0	11	11	67	72	3	2.0	7.4	55	49%	.332
2017	SAC	AAA	24	6	6	0	15	13	88^2	94	7	2.7	8.1	80	51%	.328
2018	SJO	A+	25	0	0	0	1	1	6^2	8	0	2.7	9.4	7	43%	.381
2018	SAC	AAA	25	2	0	0	3	3	16^2	10	0	3.8	8.6	16	48%	.238
2018	SFN	MLB	25	7	13	0	29	29	160^1	163	23	2.5	7.3	130	53%	.302
2019	SFN	MLB	26	5	6	0	26	15	86	84	9	2.6	7.8	75	48%	.299

Breakout: 29%   Improve: 42%   Collapse: 20%   Attrition: 28%   MLB: 80%
Comparables: Robbie Erlin, Tyler Duffey, Juan Nicasio

The easiest way to meet expectations is to never set them too high. With four pitches, none of them plus, and solid-but-unspectacular command of the lot, Suarez was billed as a back-end starter, nothing more, nothing less. He fulfilled that promise swiftly in his first big-league year, pitching to league-average results for most of the season before fatigue set in down the stretch. Suarez compensates for his lack of swing-and-miss stuff by pounding the bottom of the zone, inducing enough ground balls to keep his home-run rates in check. While his misses above the belt are vulnerable to glove-side opponents and in hitter-friendly environs, the depth of his arsenal is an asset on his third tour through the order. The former Miami Hurricane will never be mistaken for an ace, but as long as the expectations don't rise above what he was as a rookie, Suarez won't disappoint in his sophomore year.

YEAR	TEAM	LVL	AGE	WHIP	ERA	DRA	WARP	MPH	FB%	WHF	CSP
2016	SJO	A+	23	1.01	2.43	3.38	0.7				
2016	RIC	AA	23	1.34	3.95	2.90	3.0				
2017	RIC	AA	24	1.30	2.96	3.89	1.0				
2017	SAC	AAA	24	1.36	3.55	3.82	1.8				
2018	SJO	A+	25	1.50	1.35	7.07	-0.1				
2018	SAC	AAA	25	1.02	1.08	3.57	0.4				
2018	SFN	MLB	25	1.30	4.49	4.08	2.3	93.5	51.2	8.3	49.5
2019	SFN	MLB	26	1.27	3.67	4.14	0.9	93.1	52.1	8.4	50.4

Andrew Suarez, continued

Pitch Shape vs LHH

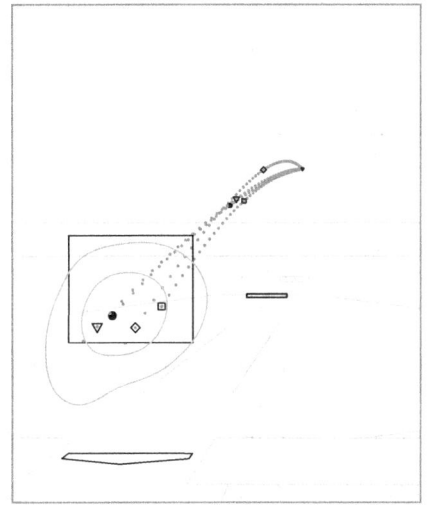

Pitch Shape vs RHH

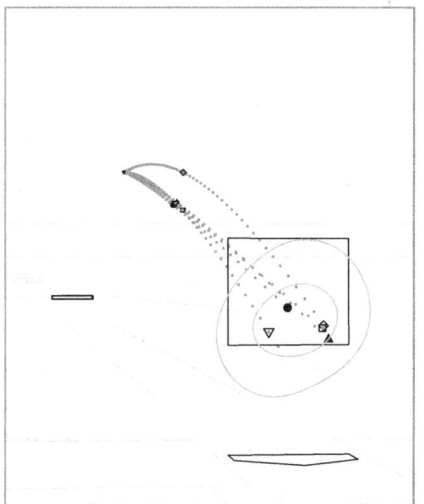

Type	Frequency	Velocity	H Movement	V Movement
● Fastball	35.9%	92.7 [101]	8.4 [92]	-15.1 [102]
□ Sinker	15.3%	92.2 [99]	11.6 [108]	-17.7 [109]
+ Cutter				
▲ Changeup	11.7%	86.4 [104]	12.5 [94]	-24.2 [109]
× Splitter				
▽ Slider	23.8%	88.9 [120]	-3.1 [92]	-26.1 [120]
◇ Curveball	13.4%	77.2 [95]	-6.7 [95]	-48.3 [99]
⊕ Slow Curveball				
✳ Knuckleball				
▼ Screwball				

Nick Vincent RHP

Born: 07/12/86 Age: 32 Bats: R Throws: R
Height: 6'0" Weight: 185 Origin: Round 18, 2008 Draft (#555 overall)

YEAR	TEAM	LVL	AGE	W	L	SV	G	GS	IP	H	HR	BB/9	K/9	K	GB%	BABIP
2016	SEA	MLB	29	4	4	3	60	0	60^1	53	11	2.2	9.7	65	34%	.271
2017	SEA	MLB	30	3	3	0	69	0	64^2	62	3	1.8	7.0	50	35%	.301
2018	SEA	MLB	31	4	4	0	62	1	56^1	50	7	2.4	8.9	56	31%	.272
2019	SFN	MLB	32	1	1	0	16	0	16	17	3	3.3	8.4	16	35%	.298

Breakout: 16%   Improve: 35%   Collapse: 30%   Attrition: 9%   MLB: 86%
Comparables: Casey Janssen, Todd Coffey, Matt Bush

Armed with the pitch arsenal, physique, and at times facial hair of a bygone era, Vincent is something like baseball's third-best bar mitzvah magician. He throws a fastball that tops out around 90 mph, a cutter about two ticks below that, and that's about it. He throws them near the top of the strike zone, to any and all manner of terrifying opposing hitter. When the magic is on, and the fly balls stay in the park, he rides those two pitches and that approach to years like 2017, when he erased eighth innings so effectively you hardly noticed them. When the balls carry over the fence, he'll still provide adequate relief, if even the mere appearance of him warming up will chill your very soul. Either way, the audience will be on the edge of their seats the entire time.

YEAR	TEAM	LVL	AGE	WHIP	ERA	DRA	WARP	MPH	FB%	WHF	CSP
2016	SEA	MLB	29	1.13	3.73	3.16	1.3	92.0	94.8	16.2	48.4
2017	SEA	MLB	30	1.16	3.20	4.11	0.8	91.3	94.4	11.2	49.3
2018	SEA	MLB	31	1.15	3.99	3.55	0.9	90.7	96	13.2	50.9
2019	SFN	MLB	32	1.39	4.83	5.06	-0.1	90.3	94.3	13.1	49.3

Nick Vincent, continued

Pitch Shape vs LHH

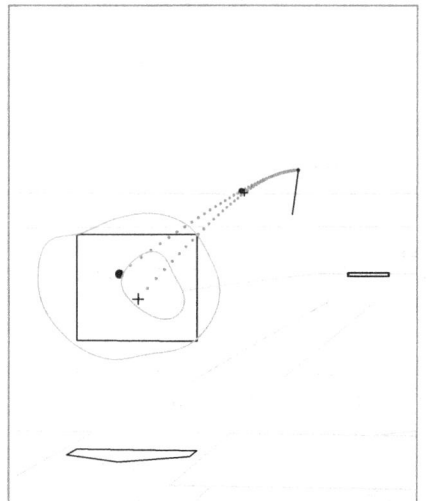

Pitch Shape vs RHH

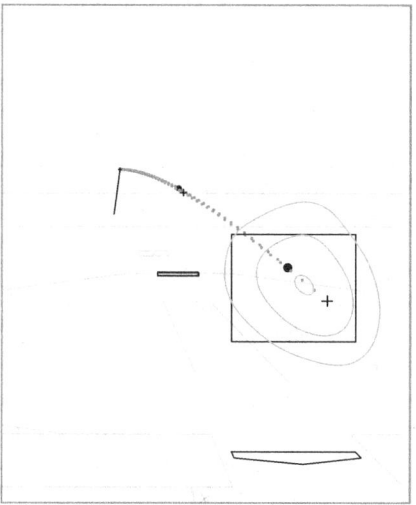

Type	Frequency	Velocity	H Movement	V Movement
● Fastball	39.0%	90.1 [92]	-3.8 [113]	-15.5 [101]
☐ Sinker	1.8%	89.9 [87]	-11.2 [112]	-20.6 [99]
+ Cutter	55.2%	88 [95]	2.5 [104]	-20.8 [112]
▲ Changeup	3.9%	84 [94]	-13.7 [87]	-28.9 [95]
✕ Splitter				
▽ Slider				
◇ Curveball	0.1%	81 [109]	4.9 [87]	-42.3 [113]
✦ Slow Curveball				
✱ Knuckleball				
▼ Screwball				

Tony Watson LHP
Born: 05/30/85   Age: 34   Bats: L   Throws: L
Height: 6'3"   Weight: 218   Origin: Round 9, 2007 Draft (#278 overall)

YEAR	TEAM	LVL	AGE	W	L	SV	G	GS	IP	H	HR	BB/9	K/9	K	GB%	BABIP
2016	PIT	MLB	31	2	5	15	70	0	67^2	52	10	2.7	7.7	58	46%	.232
2017	PIT	MLB	32	5	3	10	47	0	46^2	57	7	2.7	6.8	35	46%	.333
2017	LAN	MLB	32	2	1	0	24	0	20	15	2	2.7	8.1	18	62%	.241
2018	SFN	MLB	33	4	6	0	72	0	66	54	4	1.9	9.8	72	47%	.294
2019	*SFN*	*MLB*	*34*	*3*	*3*	*4*	*53*	*0*	*56*	*50*	*7*	*3.1*	*8.8*	*54*	*46%*	*.289*

Breakout: 9%   Improve: 27%   Collapse: 47%   Attrition: 6%   MLB: 90%
Comparables: Hideki Okajima, Joe Smith, Scot Shields

Caught up in the deflated free-agent market of 2017-2018, Watson signed for pennies on the dollar just days after pitchers and catchers reported to camp. The southpaw's financial loss was the Giants' gain, both in the bullpen and on the books, as his creatively structured deal kept his new team from incurring the luxury tax. On the mound, Watson stayed a step ahead of his opponents by tweaking his pitch mix. The 2018 edition featured fewer sinkers and more sliders, along with career-high changeup usage, all of which yielded his best strikeout rate in eight years. An impressively nimble reliever who's thrived regardless of foe, role or setting, he'll be a top setup option again this year.

YEAR	TEAM	LVL	AGE	WHIP	ERA	DRA	WARP	MPH	FB%	WHF	CSP
2016	PIT	MLB	31	1.06	3.06	4.35	0.5	95.5	66.5	13.5	46.3
2017	PIT	MLB	32	1.52	3.66	5.55	-0.2	95.0	65.1	14	50.8
2017	LAN	MLB	32	1.05	2.70	5.14	0.0	95.2	64.9	13.3	46.7
2018	SFN	MLB	33	1.03	2.59	3.31	1.2	94.2	51.2	13.9	54.4
2019	*SFN*	*MLB*	*34*	*1.24*	*3.81*	*4.26*	*0.3*	*93.7*	*58.9*	*13.6*	*50*

Tony Watson, continued

Pitch Shape vs LHH

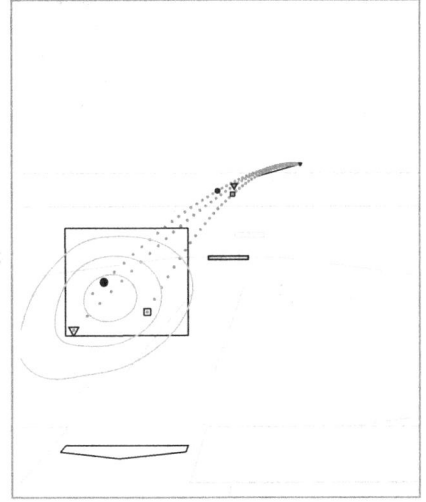

Pitch Shape vs RHH

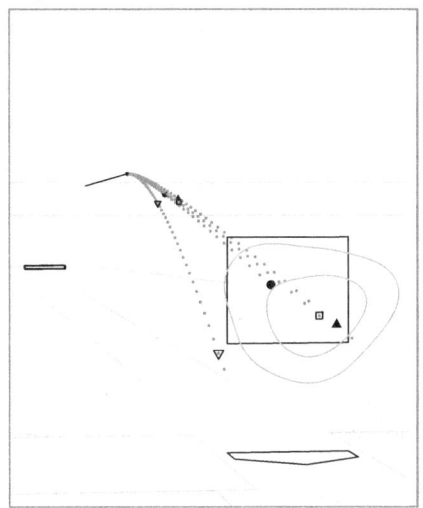

Type	Frequency	Velocity	H Movement	V Movement
● Fastball	28.6%	93.2 [102]	12.5 [73]	-19.2 [89]
□ Sinker	22.5%	92.9 [102]	16.4 [68]	-22.9 [92]
+ Cutter				
▲ Changeup	29.6%	86.1 [103]	17.4 [67]	-26.6 [102]
× Splitter				
▽ Slider	19.2%	84.6 [101]	-2.3 [89]	-31.4 [105]
◇ Curveball				
⊕ Slow Curveball				
✳ Knuckleball				
▼ Screwball				

Abiatal Avelino MI

Born: 02/14/95   Age: 24   Bats: R   Throws: R
Height: 5'11"   Weight: 195   Origin: International Free Agent, 2011

YEAR	TEAM	LVL	AGE	PA	R	2B	3B	HR	RBI	BB	K	SB	CS	AVG/OBP/SLG
2016	TAM	A+	21	394	54	17	2	6	34	29	63	20	13	.266/.325/.375
2016	TRN	AA	21	141	15	11	0	0	14	10	19	1	2	.244/.307/.331
2017	TAM	A+	22	34	1	1	0	0	2	2	5	4	0	.219/.265/.250
2017	SWB	AAA	22	68	5	1	1	0	6	5	10	3	1	.213/.284/.262
2017	TRN	AA	22	249	35	12	4	3	28	14	33	4	0	.270/.315/.396
2018	TRN	AA	23	211	32	7	2	10	28	18	37	15	4	.337/.392/.553
2018	SWB	AAA	23	290	33	6	6	5	38	14	61	10	2	.252/.291/.372
2018	SFN	MLB	23	11	1	0	0	0	0	0	3	0	0	.273/.273/.273
2019	SFN	MLB	24	72	8	3	1	2	8	3	15	2	1	.250/.282/.412

Breakout: 19%   Improve: 32%   Collapse: 1%   Attrition: 29%   MLB: 46%
Comparables: Trevor Plouffe, T.J. Rivera, Tim Beckham

A glove-first prospect until 2018, Avelino exploded offensively after a restart in Double-A, showing previously unseen power in his second stint with Trenton. Intrigued by the apparent breakout, the Giants targeted the infielder in the Andrew McCutchen trade and gave him a sip of coffee in the majors last September. Avelino's modest frame has little room for added muscle, but the newfound pop stemmed from a retooled approach, which saw the San Pedro De Macoris native reduce his ground-ball rate by 15 percentage points between his two stops in Double-A. Couple that with Avelino's plus arm and slick infield actions, and you can see the makings of a second-division regular at short. If the launch-angle gains don't hold up to major-league pitching, Avelino can always fall back on his versatility, serving as a capable backup anywhere on the dirt.

YEAR	TEAM	LVL	AGE	PA	DRC+	VORP	BABIP	BRR	FRAA	WARP
2016	TAM	A+	21	394	110	10.1	.305	0.4	2B(44): 1.0, SS(43): -1.0	0.9
2016	TRN	AA	21	141	87	1.8	.284	0.8	2B(23): 0.4, SS(9): -0.8	0.1
2017	TAM	A+	22	34	69	-0.8	.259	0.6	3B(8): 0.5, 2B(2): 0.0	0.0
2017	SWB	AAA	22	68	61	-1.6	.255	0.1	SS(11): 0.0, 3B(6): -0.4	-0.2
2017	TRN	AA	22	249	91	12.7	.301	4.4	2B(39): 1.7, SS(16): 0.5	0.7
2018	TRN	AA	23	211	157	26.5	.375	-0.2	SS(44): 3.4, 2B(2): 0.3	2.3
2018	SWB	AAA	23	290	64	1.3	.308	1.7	SS(52): 3.4, 2B(16): 2.2	0.3
2018	SFN	MLB	23	11	75	0.0	.375	0.2	SS(3): 0.0, 2B(1): -0.1	0.0
2019	SFN	MLB	24	72	78	1.1	.268	0.2	SS 1, 2B 0	0.2

Joey Bart C

Born: 12/15/96 Age: 22 Bats: R Throws: R
Height: 6'3" Weight: 220 Origin: Round 1, 2018 Draft (#2 overall)

YEAR	TEAM	LVL	AGE	PA	R	2B	3B	HR	RBI	BB	K	SB	CS	AVG/OBP/SLG
2018	GNT	RK	21	25	3	1	1	0	1	1	7	0	0	.261/.320/.391
2018	SLO	A-	21	203	35	14	2	13	39	12	40	2	1	.298/.369/.613
2019	SFN	MLB	22	251	23	10	0	12	32	5	74	0	0	.157/.192/.346

Breakout: 3% Improve: 10% Collapse: 0% Attrition: 8% MLB: 12%
Comparables: J.T. Realmuto, Austin Hedges, Blake Swihart

John Barr, a 33-year veteran of baseball front offices, led the Giants' amateur draft room for 11 years, beginning with the first-round selection of Buster Posey in 2008. Since the 2013 draft, however, only 10 of Barr's choices have even reached the majors, and the leading WARP-getter among them was Andrew Suarez, who just debuted last year. In what would be his last draft at the helm, Barr held the Giants' earliest selection since 1985 at second overall. There, Barr chose another potential franchise cornerstone catcher: Bart, whose combination of power at the plate and polish behind it earned him a spot atop the team's board. Signed to a record $7.025 million bonus, Bart tormented short-season arms, but his true offensive potential won't be known until he proves his contact skills in Double-A. With little doubt about his bat speed or aptitude in the squat, Bart's hit tool—below average at present with average potential—will determine whether he's a rich or poor man's Mike Zunino.

YEAR	TEAM	LVL	AGE	PA	DRC+	VORP	BABIP	BRR	FRAA	WARP
2018	GNT	RK	21	25	83	0.6	.375	-0.1	C(4): -0.1	0.0
2018	SLO	A-	21	203	147	21.6	.318	1.2	C(32): -1.0	1.0
2019	SFN	MLB	22	251	39	-8.2	.171	-0.4	C -1	-0.9

Alexander Canario CF

Born: 05/07/00   Age: 19   Bats: R   Throws: R
Height: 6'1"   Weight: 165   Origin: International Free Agent, 2016

YEAR	TEAM	LVL	AGE	PA	R	2B	3B	HR	RBI	BB	K	SB	CS	AVG/OBP/SLG
2017	DGI	RK	17	274	42	17	4	5	45	33	40	18	10	.294/.391/.464
2018	GIA	RK	18	208	36	5	2	6	19	27	51	8	5	.250/.357/.403
2019	SFN	MLB	19	251	20	8	0	6	23	12	86	3	2	.152/.190/.269

Breakout: 6%   Improve: 8%   Collapse: 0%   Attrition: 3%   MLB: 10%
Comparables: Nomar Mazara, Engel Beltre, Gleyber Torres

The league's best farm systems have a flock of Canarios, and sometimes, a couple soar above the crowd. As one of the few tooled-up teenagers on the Giants farm, the 18-year-old was the headliner on the club's two Arizona League affiliates, and he didn't disappoint. Signed for just $60,000 three years ago, he's athletic and swings the bat with authority, projecting for above-average power while showing the speed to handle center. The latter may diminish with increased age and muscle but added strength might push his raw pop to plus, enough for everyday work in a corner. Canario's hit tool is nascent, his offense entirely based around punishing fastballs, but the ingredients of an impact bat are present, and that's more than scouts could say for his AZL teammates. He has star-level upside as a center fielder, with the extreme volatility that makes you wish you had more birds of his feather.

YEAR	TEAM	LVL	AGE	PA	DRC+	VORP	BABIP	BRR	FRAA	WARP
2017	DGI	RK	17	274	164	24.0	.335	-1.0	RF(50): 4.0, CF(7): 0.7	2.2
2018	GIA	RK	18	208	114	13.2	.317	-0.5	CF(44): 1.0	0.4
2019	SFN	MLB	19	251	20	-14.6	.200	-0.2	CF -1	-1.6

Sandro Fabian RF
Born: 03/06/98 Age: 21 Bats: R Throws: R
Height: 6'1" Weight: 180 Origin: International Free Agent, 2015

YEAR	TEAM	LVL	AGE	PA	R	2B	3B	HR	RBI	BB	K	SB	CS	AVG/OBP/SLG
2016	GIA	RK	18	174	30	13	5	2	35	7	28	3	1	.340/.364/.522
2017	AUG	A	19	504	51	30	0	11	61	10	88	5	4	.277/.297/.408
2018	SJO	A+	20	450	47	19	1	10	35	26	107	1	2	.200/.260/.325
2019	SFN	MLB	21	251	18	9	0	7	26	1	69	0	0	.182/.187/.305

Breakout: 2% Improve: 4% Collapse: 0% Attrition: 4% MLB: 4%
Comparables: Kyle Waldrop, Moises Sierra, Rymer Liriano

Sending Fabian to High-A at the start of 2018 was tantamount to throwing a toddler into the ocean the moment he stops screaming in the tub. The Giants' overzealous parenting, prompted by Fabian treading water in the Sally League at 19, left one of their top outfield prospects flailing like a wounded fish in San Jose. Fabian's slump was predictable based on his chase rate in the box and, considering the Giants never threw him a life preserver, perhaps they felt the kid outfielder needed to learn selectivity the hard way. He didn't, and the struggles highlighted both his distance from the majors and the significant risk tied to his approach. Fabian may yet surface as a second-division regular whose batting average compensates for his low walk totals, but both the odds and the timeframe are much longer than they seemed last year.

YEAR	TEAM	LVL	AGE	PA	DRC+	VORP	BABIP	BRR	FRAA	WARP
2016	GIA	RK	18	174	150	15.9	.388	-1.3	RF(40): 2.9, LF(1): -0.1	0.5
2017	AUG	A	19	504	119	10.0	.317	-1.5	RF(111): 21.5, CF(2): -0.7	3.1
2018	SJO	A+	20	450	59	-8.7	.241	-1.7	RF(112): 3.7	-1.9
2019	SFN	MLB	21	251	24	-16.7	.217	-0.6	RF 4	-1.3

San Francisco Giants 2019

Mike Gerber   RF

Born: 07/08/92   Age: 26   Bats: L   Throws: R
Height: 6'0"   Weight: 190   Origin: Round 15, 2014 Draft (#460 overall)

YEAR	TEAM	LVL	AGE	PA	R	2B	3B	HR	RBI	BB	K	SB	CS	AVG/OBP/SLG
2016	LAK	A+	23	388	52	22	3	14	60	32	111	2	3	.282/.343/.481
2016	ERI	AA	23	175	17	8	3	4	20	20	41	6	0	.261/.349/.431
2017	ERI	AA	24	394	62	22	2	13	45	39	85	10	6	.291/.363/.477
2018	DET	MLB	25	47	2	1	0	0	2	4	21	0	0	.095/.170/.119
2018	TOL	AAA	25	316	35	14	2	13	34	22	103	2	2	.213/.277/.411
2019	SFN	MLB	26	251	26	11	1	8	30	17	76	2	1	.210/.268/.375

Breakout: 6%   Improve: 32%   Collapse: 7%   Attrition: 29%   MLB: 53%
Comparables: Blake Tekotte, Corey Brown, Matt Den Dekker

Gerber hangs right on the bell curve across the breadth of the outfielder skill set. He might remind you of Andy Dirks in that regard, or the Valkyrie from *Gauntlet*, reliable for any purpose but not for one. If you hold up his numbers, his minor-league progression looked quite promising, assuming you held your thumb over the 2018 line, which was a clever parlor trick on your part. Gerber's first taste of the majors ate him alive (as if the 50 percent strikeout rate wasn't telling enough) and he was understandably not recalled when rosters expanded in September. He's still a power threat who can play some center field, which is always enough to contend for a fourth outfielder spot.

YEAR	TEAM	LVL	AGE	PA	DRC+	VORP	BABIP	BRR	FRAA	WARP
2016	LAK	A+	23	388	126	13.3	.371	-0.6	RF(61): 1.3, CF(16): -0.9	1.0
2016	ERI	AA	23	175	94	7.9	.330	0.8	CF(20): -2.1, RF(19): 2.0	0.1
2017	ERI	AA	24	394	127	27.5	.349	1.2	CF(87): -6.8	1.0
2018	DET	MLB	25	47	51	-5.7	.182	-0.2	LF(7): -1.2, CF(4): 2.3	-0.1
2018	TOL	AAA	25	316	76	1.1	.279	-0.9	CF(40): -3.4, RF(28): 0.2	-0.9
2019	SFN	MLB	26	251	75	0.7	.269	-0.2	CF 0, RF 0	0.0

Jacob Gonzalez 3B

Born: 06/26/98 Age: 21 Bats: R Throws: R
Height: 6'3" Weight: 190 Origin: Round 2, 2017 Draft (#58 overall)

YEAR	TEAM	LVL	AGE	PA	R	2B	3B	HR	RBI	BB	K	SB	CS	AVG/OBP/SLG
2017	GIA	RK	19	194	23	15	1	1	21	16	23	0	1	.339/.418/.458
2018	AUG	A	20	507	54	20	2	8	45	31	107	7	5	.227/.296/.331
2019	SFN	MLB	21	251	18	9	0	5	23	4	68	0	0	.174/.202/.278

Breakout: 0% Improve: 1% Collapse: 0% Attrition: 1% MLB: 1%
Comparables: Jefry Marte, Jeimer Candelario, Cheslor Cuthbert

A polished hitter for his age, Gonzalez is young enough that his Sally League stumble is more cause for caution than concern. The son of former slugger Luis Gonzalez, Jacob gears his swing for maximum power, using a high knee-lift to gather and explosive hip rotation to hammer the ball to left. While his raw pop is undeniable, its utility is tempered by a tendency to pull off of pitches away, a hole that Low-A arms gladly exposed. Gonzalez is a hard worker who should improve with time, but effort may not be enough to keep him at third base, where his awkward actions portend a move to first or left. Either would amplify the pressure on his hit tool, making Gonzalez a high-risk potential average regular who's more likely to end up a four-corners reserve.

YEAR	TEAM	LVL	AGE	PA	DRC+	VORP	BABIP	BRR	FRAA	WARP
2017	GIA	RK	19	194	190	17.6	.384	-2.1	3B(39): -6.2	0.3
2018	AUG	A	20	507	91	3.4	.277	-3.4	3B(94): -6.4	-1.1
2019	SFN	MLB	21	251	24	-17.8	.219	-0.5	3B -3	-2.2

San Francisco Giants 2019

Ryan Howard INF
Born: 07/25/94   Age: 24   Bats: R   Throws: R
Height: 6'2"   Weight: 195   Origin: Round 5, 2016 Draft (#155 overall)

YEAR	TEAM	LVL	AGE	PA	R	2B	3B	HR	RBI	BB	K	SB	CS	AVG/OBP/SLG
2016	SLO	A-	21	246	33	10	0	4	31	13	24	2	2	.272/.313/.371
2017	SJO	A+	22	565	59	21	0	9	50	23	81	7	2	.306/.342/.397
2018	RIC	AA	23	475	44	32	4	4	50	39	55	9	5	.273/.336/.396
2019	SFN	MLB	24	37	4	1	0	1	3	2	6	0	0	.200/.243/.314

Breakout: 26%   Improve: 36%   Collapse: 1%   Attrition: 33%   MLB: 49%
Comparables: Kevin Newman, Adam Frazier, David Fletcher

Promoted from hitter-friendly San Jose to the pitchers' haven of Richmond, Howard doubled his walk rate while reducing his strikeouts, displaying the sort of strike-zone management that catches scouts' attention when one's physical tools don't. The Mizzou product can shoot the gaps, placing third in the Eastern League in doubles, but he's content to punch the ball the other way, missing the approach and lower-half explosiveness to bop more than a handful of homers a year. In the field, Howard has just enough range at short but fits better at second, where his solid-average arm would be an asset in various defensive shifts. If that reads like a utility profile, well, it is, and Howard could be in line for such work by midyear.

YEAR	TEAM	LVL	AGE	PA	DRC+	VORP	BABIP	BRR	FRAA	WARP
2016	SLO	A-	21	246	95	7.4	.285	0.0	SS(58): -12.0	-1.2
2017	SJO	A+	22	565	115	29.4	.345	-0.3	SS(101): -9.7, 3B(23): -4.6	0.1
2018	RIC	AA	23	475	116	27.3	.302	0.5	SS(93): -7.6, 2B(21): -5.7	0.7
2019	SFN	MLB	24	37	40	-1.4	.245	0.0	2B -1	-0.3

Jalen Miller 2B

Born: 12/19/96 Age: 22 Bats: R Throws: R
Height: 5'11" Weight: 190 Origin: Round 3, 2015 Draft (#95 overall)

YEAR	TEAM	LVL	AGE	PA	R	2B	3B	HR	RBI	BB	K	SB	CS	AVG/OBP/SLG
2016	AUG	A	19	500	65	20	5	5	44	26	107	11	5	.223/.271/.322
2017	SJO	A+	20	470	61	25	4	6	44	31	100	6	4	.227/.283/.346
2018	SJO	A+	21	554	73	35	2	14	62	27	121	11	4	.276/.321/.434
2019	SFN	MLB	22	251	23	9	0	6	21	6	68	1	1	.176/.198/.293

Breakout: 7% Improve: 9% Collapse: 0% Attrition: 5% MLB: 9%
Comparables: Charlie Culberson, Rey Navarro, Jeff Bianchi

Miller announced his breakout intentions by hitting for the cycle in his seventh game of the season, an 18-6 Lancaster special in which his teammate, Gio Brusa, did the same. By year's end, the athletic infielder led all Giants farmhands in extra-base hits and was named High-A San Jose's team MVP. There are plenty of caveats to Miller's newfound power—he was repeating the level as a 21-year-old, it was the Cal League, he struggled with spin—but the glass-half-full view shows a toolsy young player finding his bearings at the plate. Miller is already a nifty defender at the keystone and he runs well underway, so if the bat blooms late, he could play every day. He'll be out to prove the legitimacy of his power as he advances to Double-A.

YEAR	TEAM	LVL	AGE	PA	DRC+	VORP	BABIP	BRR	FRAA	WARP
2016	AUG	A	19	500	72	3.5	.277	3.8	2B(104): -6.2, SS(7): -0.6	-1.4
2017	SJO	A+	20	470	71	2.4	.281	1.2	2B(83): -9.0, SS(28): -0.6	-2.0
2018	SJO	A+	21	554	108	34.4	.335	1.5	2B(119): -9.7	-0.3
2019	SFN	MLB	22	251	25	-14.4	.213	-0.3	2B -3	-1.9

Heath Quinn OF

Born: 06/07/95   Age: 24   Bats: R   Throws: R
Height: 6'3"   Weight: 220   Origin: Round 3, 2016 Draft (#95 overall)

YEAR	TEAM	LVL	AGE	PA	R	2B	3B	HR	RBI	BB	K	SB	CS	AVG/OBP/SLG
2016	SLO	A-	21	239	37	19	1	9	34	26	50	3	0	.337/.423/.571
2017	SJO	A+	22	297	24	9	0	10	29	20	86	0	0	.228/.290/.371
2018	SJO	A+	23	407	53	24	0	14	51	42	98	4	1	.300/.376/.485
2019	SFN	MLB	24	251	23	8	0	8	29	14	79	0	0	.197/.245/.339

Breakout: 6%   Improve: 8%   Collapse: 0%   Attrition: 9%   MLB: 12%
Comparables: Jake Cave, Marc Krauss, Jaycob Brugman

A fractured hamate and a bum shoulder are any power hitter's worst nightmare, and Quinn endured both in 2017. Healthy again to begin last season, he excelled in a repeat tour of the Cal League, exhibiting the physicality and all-fields thunder that made him a third-round pick three years ago. With a plus arm accompanying his pop, Quinn checks the boxes that a right-field prospect must, and though he's more strongman than speedster, he won't be a hindrance on the grass. Assuming the injury bug flies away, Quinn's strikeout rate will dictate if he's a second-division regular or a short-end platooner who stars in BP.

YEAR	TEAM	LVL	AGE	PA	DRC+	VORP	BABIP	BRR	FRAA	WARP
2016	SLO	A-	21	239	176	26.9	.405	1.7	RF(49): 11.2	2.5
2017	SJO	A+	22	297	72	-2.6	.294	-2.8	RF(35): -0.5, LF(26): -7.4	-2.2
2018	SJO	A+	23	407	143	30.9	.373	0.3	LF(58): -11.4	0.3
2019	SFN	MLB	24	251	52	-8.2	.255	-0.5	LF -7, RF 0	-1.6

Heliot Ramos CF

Born: 09/07/99 Age: 19 Bats: R Throws: R
Height: 6'2" Weight: 185 Origin: Round 1, 2017 Draft (#19 overall)

YEAR	TEAM	LVL	AGE	PA	R	2B	3B	HR	RBI	BB	K	SB	CS	AVG/OBP/SLG
2017	GIA	RK	17	151	33	11	6	6	27	10	48	10	2	.348/.404/.645
2018	AUG	A	18	535	61	24	8	11	52	35	136	8	7	.245/.313/.396
2019	SFN	MLB	19	251	22	9	2	7	24	3	92	1	0	.176/.186/.321

Breakout: 7% Improve: 9% Collapse: 0% Attrition: 3% MLB: 11%
Comparables: Engel Beltre, Nomar Mazara, Gleyber Torres

The Giants prefer to challenge rather than coddle their prospects, so a stellar pro debut in the Arizona League netted Ramos a chance to impress as the youngest player in the Sally. That context is critical when evaluating his performance, and while the topline numbers were pedestrian, his tools are anything but. Ramos converted his plus raw power into 43 extra-base hits and he placed fourth in the circuit with eight triples, utilizing the speed that will also enable him to stay in center field. While the Puerto Rican has bat speed to spare, his nascent approach is an area for improvement. A gap-to-gap hitter at present, scouts believe Ramos will develop selective aggression, learning to identify pitches he can pull over the fence and ones he's better off watching go by. Like any teenager, Ramos will need a few years of trial and error to find his place in the world. He could be a first-division regular if all breaks right.

YEAR	TEAM	LVL	AGE	PA	DRC+	VORP	BABIP	BRR	FRAA	WARP
2017	GIA	RK	17	151	178	20.8	.500	2.2	CF(29): -2.3	0.7
2018	AUG	A	18	535	107	21.5	.319	1.8	CF(113): -4.5	0.7
2019	SFN	MLB	19	251	27	-12.7	.242	-0.1	CF -1	-1.5

San Francisco Giants 2019

Chris Shaw LF
Born: 10/20/93 Age: 25 Bats: L Throws: R
Height: 6'3" Weight: 226 Origin: Round 1, 2015 Draft (#31 overall)

YEAR	TEAM	LVL	AGE	PA	R	2B	3B	HR	RBI	BB	K	SB	CS	AVG/OBP/SLG
2016	SJO	A+	22	305	47	22	0	16	55	28	70	0	0	.285/.357/.544
2016	RIC	AA	22	256	26	16	4	5	30	20	55	0	0	.246/.309/.414
2017	RIC	AA	23	154	16	10	0	6	29	18	26	0	0	.301/.390/.511
2017	SAC	AAA	23	360	42	25	1	18	50	20	106	0	0	.289/.328/.530
2018	SAC	AAA	24	422	55	21	2	24	65	21	144	0	0	.259/.308/.505
2018	SFN	MLB	24	62	2	2	0	1	7	7	23	1	0	.185/.274/.278
2019	SFN	MLB	25	239	29	13	1	10	29	10	74	0	0	.227/.264/.427

Breakout: 10%   Improve: 26%   Collapse: 3%   Attrition: 27%   MLB: 46%
Comparables: Matt Clark, Andrew Lambo, Daniel Dorn

In Shaw's case, power isn't everything ... it's the only thing. The Boston College product can top the light-tower, but he's a 30-grade runner, merely acceptable at first base and unable to cover the outfield gaps. For players with this profile, contact rate draws the line between Quad-A slugger and second-division player in the bigs. Shaw toed the wrong side of it last season, both in Triple-A and in his major-league debut, where he swung at 42 percent of pitches outside of the strike zone. While jumpiness is normal for a rookie trying too hard to impress, pitchers were thrilled to find him equally willing to expand on fastballs up and sliders down, and the prolific chase rate poses a grave threat to Shaw's primary tool. The former first-round pick can be productive if he just strikes out one-fourth of the time instead of one-third, but he's yet to put bat on ball consistently above Double-A.

YEAR	TEAM	LVL	AGE	PA	DRC+	VORP	BABIP	BRR	FRAA	WARP
2016	SJO	A+	22	305	156	24.7	.326	-2.4	1B(52): -0.9	0.9
2016	RIC	AA	22	256	93	1.6	.299	-3.5	1B(48): -2.3	-1.0
2017	RIC	AA	23	154	150	10.5	.333	-1.5	1B(18): -0.9, LF(18): -1.1	0.4
2017	SAC	AAA	23	360	98	13.4	.367	-5.3	LF(76): -14.5	-1.6
2018	SAC	AAA	24	422	103	14.4	.345	-2.0	LF(86): -10.4	-0.6
2018	SFN	MLB	24	62	65	-1.8	.290	-0.1	LF(15): -1.9	-0.3
2019	SFN	MLB	25	239	83	1.6	.289	-0.3	LF -2, RF 0	-0.2

Shaun Anderson RHP

Born: 10/29/94 Age: 24 Bats: R Throws: R
Height: 6'4" Weight: 225 Origin: Round 3, 2016 Draft (#88 overall)

YEAR	TEAM	LVL	AGE	W	L	SV	G	GS	IP	H	HR	BB/9	K/9	K	GB%	BABIP
2017	GRN	A	22	3	0	0	7	7	38²	30	2	2.6	8.6	37	52%	.272
2017	SLM	A+	22	3	3	0	11	11	58²	53	6	2.8	7.4	48	43%	.270
2017	SJO	A+	22	3	3	0	6	5	25²	19	1	1.4	7.7	22	51%	.247
2018	RIC	AA	23	6	5	0	17	16	94	93	9	2.1	8.9	93	49%	.316
2018	SAC	AAA	23	2	2	0	8	8	47¹	48	5	2.1	6.5	34	47%	.287
2019	SFN	MLB	24	1	1	0	3	3	15	15	2	2.7	7.8	14	44%	.294

Breakout: 11% Improve: 22% Collapse: 20% Attrition: 39% MLB: 51%
Comparables: Walker Lockett, Simon Castro, Matt Andriese

During his junior year at the University of Florida, Anderson shared a roster with six future first- or second-rounders. That collection of arms relegated him to the bullpen as a collegian, his four-pitch repertoire and starter's motion notwithstanding. The Red Sox saw a mid-rotation arm when they chose Anderson in the third round in 2016, and the Giants, who obtained the right-hander in the Eduardo Nunez trade, heartily agree. While Anderson doesn't have a putaway pitch, he manipulates the shape of his slider and the depth of his changeup, keeping each offering in a distinct velocity band to turn over lineups multiple times. Add an ideal pitcher's frame and easy mechanics, and you've got a near-ready fourth starter. Anderson should shed the "near" part this year.

YEAR	TEAM	LVL	AGE	WHIP	ERA	DRA	WARP	MPH	FB%	WHF	CSP
2017	GRN	A	22	1.06	2.56	3.62	0.8				
2017	SLM	A+	22	1.21	3.99	3.80	1.0				
2017	SJO	A+	22	0.90	3.51	4.63	0.2				
2018	RIC	AA	23	1.22	3.45	2.88	2.7				
2018	SAC	AAA	23	1.25	4.18	4.09	0.8				
2019	SFN	MLB	24	1.26	4.03	4.51	0.1				

Tyler Beede   RHP

Born: 05/23/93   Age: 26   Bats: R   Throws: R
Height: 6'3"   Weight: 211   Origin: Round 1, 2014 Draft (#14 overall)

YEAR	TEAM	LVL	AGE	W	L	SV	G	GS	IP	H	HR	BB/9	K/9	K	GB%	BABIP
2016	RIC	AA	23	8	7	0	24	24	147^1	136	9	3.2	8.2	135	49%	.309
2017	SAC	AAA	24	6	7	0	19	19	109	121	14	3.2	6.9	83	52%	.316
2018	SFN	MLB	25	0	1	0	2	2	7^2	9	0	9.4	10.6	9	46%	.409
2018	SAC	AAA	25	4	9	0	33	10	74	82	10	6.8	9.1	75	41%	.346
2019	*SFN*	*MLB*	*26*	*1*	*2*	*0*	*5*	*5*	*25*	*23*	*3*	*4.3*	*8.6*	*24*	*44%*	*.295*

Breakout: 10%   Improve: 17%   Collapse: 7%   Attrition: 22%   MLB: 32%
Comparables: Justin Haley, Tom Koehler, Chris Stratton

On draft day in 2014, most saw Beede and the Giants as a match made in heaven: a wayward ace meeting a team known for getting lost arms back on track. But instead of finding the straight and narrow up to San Fran, Beede wound up on a winding road to the Triple-A bullpen, travel time four years, severe traffic along his route. At alternating times in his pro career, Beede's control, stuff, confidence and mechanics have abandoned him. When they seemed to gel in 2016, the acquisition of Matt Moore blocked his path. That all reads like the prelude to a change of scenery, which would be a bitterly ironic ending to a marriage that seemed perfect at the start.

YEAR	TEAM	LVL	AGE	WHIP	ERA	DRA	WARP	MPH	FB%	WHF	CSP
2016	RIC	AA	23	1.28	2.81	3.17	3.4				
2017	SAC	AAA	24	1.47	4.79	5.50	0.2				
2018	SFN	MLB	25	2.22	8.22	4.22	0.1	94.3	51.8	11.5	41.3
2018	SAC	AAA	25	1.86	7.05	5.04	0.3				
2019	*SFN*	*MLB*	*26*	*1.41*	*4.23*	*4.72*	*0.1*	*93.9*	*52.7*	*11.7*	*42.1*

Seth Corry LHP

Born: 11/03/98 Age: 20 Bats: L Throws: L
Height: 6'2" Weight: 195 Origin: Round 3, 2017 Draft (#96 overall)

YEAR	TEAM	LVL	AGE	W	L	SV	G	GS	IP	H	HR	BB/9	K/9	K	GB%	BABIP
2017	GIA	RK	18	0	2	0	13	10	24^1	14	1	8.1	7.8	21	46%	.203
2018	GNT	RK	19	3	1	0	9	9	38	38	1	4.0	9.9	42	46%	.349
2018	SLO	A-	19	1	2	0	5	5	19^2	14	1	6.9	7.8	17	54%	.245
2019	SFN	MLB	20	2	5	0	11	11	40	42	6	9.5	7.6	34	43%	.317

Comparables: Jordan Hicks, Paul Blackburn, Adrian Houser

From the unique rock formations of Bryce Canyon to the breathtaking red cliffs of Zion, Utah has a national park for every outdoorsman. Indeed, it claims more national parks (five) than drafted pitchers who've eclipsed 5.0 career WARP in the major leagues. Chosen in the third round in 2017, Corry came equipped with a cutting mid-90s fastball and a plus curve, a fine starter kit to which he recently added a promising change. Now, consistency is the steepest hill the southpaw must climb—game to game, inning to inning, even pitch to pitch. There's a mountain of switchbacks between Corry and a big-league rotation, but sometimes the view at the top is worth the grueling hike.

YEAR	TEAM	LVL	AGE	WHIP	ERA	DRA	WARP	MPH	FB%	WHF	CSP
2017	GIA	RK	18	1.48	5.55	4.49	0.4				
2018	GNT	RK	19	1.45	2.61	3.69	1.0				
2018	SLO	A-	19	1.47	5.49	4.82	0.1				
2019	SFN	MLB	20	2.10	6.88	7.98	-1.2				

San Francisco Giants 2019

Camilo Doval   RHP
Born: 07/04/97   Age: 21   Bats: R   Throws: R
Height: 6'2"   Weight: 185   Origin: International Free Agent, 2015

YEAR	TEAM	LVL	AGE	W	L	SV	G	GS	IP	H	HR	BB/9	K/9	K	GB%	BABIP
2016	DGI	RK	18	2	0	1	12	0	21^2	13	0	4.6	10.0	24	64%	.260
2017	GIA	RK	19	1	2	1	17	0	32^1	23	0	3.6	14.2	51	65%	.348
2018	AUG	A	20	0	3	11	44	0	53	40	2	4.6	13.2	78	42%	.322
2019	SFN	MLB	21	2	1	1	38	0	40^1	36	5	6.8	10.3	46	47%	.318

Breakout: 0%   Improve: 0%   Collapse: 1%   Attrition: 2%   MLB: 2%
Comparables: Craig Kimbrel, Nick Goody, Alejandro Chacin

Everyone's entitled to a bad day or three, and if you forgive Doval's awful beginning of 2018, which saw him walk eight of his first 19 foes, you'll uncover one of the most exciting relievers to grace a Low-A roster last year. The Dominican's lightning-quick arm unfurls high-90s velocity and a wicked cutter, along with a slider that could tighten into a third out pitch. What holds Doval back is a slender frame that's incompatible with his max-effort motion, the source of the command deficiency and velocity variance that give scouts pause. Having just turned 21 on the Fourth of July, Doval has plenty of time to add good weight and find an answer for left-handed opponents. With a 70-grade cutter in hand, he could soar to the big leagues as soon as everything clicks.

YEAR	TEAM	LVL	AGE	WHIP	ERA	DRA	WARP	MPH	FB%	WHF	CSP
2016	DGI	RK	18	1.11	1.66	1.88	0.8				
2017	GIA	RK	19	1.11	3.90	1.58	1.4				
2018	AUG	A	20	1.26	3.06	2.85	1.2				
2019	SFN	MLB	21	1.64	5.01	5.80	-0.5				

Sean Hjelle   RHP
Born: 05/07/97   Age: 22   Bats: R   Throws: R
Height: 6'11"   Weight: 225   Origin: Round 2, 2018 Draft (#45 overall)

YEAR	TEAM	LVL	AGE	W	L	SV	G	GS	IP	H	HR	BB/9	K/9	K	GB%	BABIP
2018	SLO	A-	21	0	0	0	12	12	21^1	24	4	1.7	9.3	22	49%	.317
2019	SFN	MLB	22	2	3	0	10	10	34^2	38	6	3.2	7.2	28	39%	.316

Comparables: Eric Lauer, Matt Hall, Madison Younginer

Hoping to boost a system with few standout prospects, the Giants spent their second-round selection on a potential mid-rotation starter who literally stands out in any crowd. Hjelle—whose Norwegian surname is pronounced "jelly"—generates extraordinary extension toward the plate thanks to his beanstalk physique without exhibiting the mechanical volatility that often fells pitchers his height. Little else about the Minnesotan is exceptional, however, and he'll need to progress his modest pitch mix through further gains in the weight room. Without another tick or two across the board, Hjelle might be just an ordinary pitcher who happens to tower over his peers.

YEAR	TEAM	LVL	AGE	WHIP	ERA	DRA	WARP	MPH	FB%	WHF	CSP
2018	SLO	A-	21	1.31	5.06	2.92	0.6				
2019	SFN	MLB	22	1.47	5.21	6.03	-0.3				

Aaron Phillips RHP

Born: 10/11/96 Age: 22 Bats: R Throws: R
Height: 6'5" Weight: 215 Origin: Round 9, 2017 Draft (#276 overall)

YEAR	TEAM	LVL	AGE	W	L	SV	G	GS	IP	H	HR	BB/9	K/9	K	GB%	BABIP
2017	SLO	A-	20	3	0	1	14	0	28^1	20	2	4.1	11.4	36	47%	.265
2018	AUG	A	21	6	7	0	19	18	101^2	94	13	1.4	10.6	120	46%	.301
2019	*SFN*	*MLB*	*22*	*4*	*4*	*1*	*29*	*11*	*76^2*	*74*	*11*	*3.3*	*8.8*	*75*	*40%*	*.312*

Breakout: 15% Improve: 21% Collapse: 5% Attrition: 12% MLB: 28%
Comparables: Alec Asher, Johnny Cueto, Simon Castro

Phillips hails from upstate New York, where he endured snowy winters from birth through college. He was a three-sport high-school athlete who also played football and hoops. Even after settling on baseball at St. Bonaventure, he split his time between the outfield and the mound. In other words, this 2017 ninth-rounder checks all the boxes of a potential late-bloomer. While his changeup and command are works in progress, Phillips has the frame and mechanics of a starter, and his two best pitches—a fastball that rides above barrels and a curveball that dives below them—are increasingly en vogue. The chief constraint here is velocity, since the 91s on top-100 lists are sliders nowadays, but Phillips could settle into the back of a rotation after a few more years of focus on his primary craft.

YEAR	TEAM	LVL	AGE	WHIP	ERA	DRA	WARP	MPH	FB%	WHF	CSP
2017	SLO	A-	20	1.16	4.45	2.68	0.7				
2018	AUG	A	21	1.08	3.72	3.09	2.5				
2019	*SFN*	*MLB*	*22*	*1.34*	*4.34*	*5.04*	*0.1*				

Gregory Santos   RHP

Born: 08/28/99   Age: 19   Bats: R   Throws: R
Height: 6'2"   Weight: 190   Origin: International Free Agent, 2015

YEAR	TEAM	LVL	AGE	W	L	SV	G	GS	IP	H	HR	BB/9	K/9	K	GB%	BABIP
2016	DRX	RK	16	3	3	1	16	10	41	40	1	5.7	5.5	25	62%	.300
2017	DRS	RK	17	2	0	0	8	8	30^1	22	0	4.5	7.1	24	83%	.265
2017	DGI	RK	17	1	0	0	4	4	18^2	21	2	2.4	8.2	17	59%	.322
2018	SLO	A-	18	2	5	0	12	12	49^2	64	3	2.7	8.3	46	63%	.379
2019	SFN	MLB	19	2	4	0	11	11	42	47	6	5.8	6.2	29	55%	.318

Comparables: Jenrry Mejia, John Barbato, Alberto Cabrera

Whereas most teams favor athletic, projectable pitchers on the international market, the Giants love them some arm strength, so they jumped at the chance to acquire Santos in the Eduardo Nunez trade two summers ago. Originally signed by the Red Sox, the teenage righty wields a world-class cannon, sitting in the mid-90s while spinning a plus vertical slider to boot. That tandem alone could put Santos on the express train to the big-league bullpen, but some see a future starter if he stops to find a changeup and refine his command on the way. Like most hurlers with elite arm talent and only average athleticism, Santos is prone to losing his delivery; his particular vice is throwing across his front side. Scouts are mixed on whether it's curable, but they're unanimously fond of the arm either way.

YEAR	TEAM	LVL	AGE	WHIP	ERA	DRA	WARP	MPH	FB%	WHF	CSP
2016	DRX	RK	16	1.61	4.17	6.71	-0.5				
2017	DRS	RK	17	1.22	0.89	4.88	0.4				
2017	DGI	RK	17	1.39	1.93	4.32	0.4				
2018	SLO	A-	18	1.59	4.53	5.00	0.1				
2019	SFN	MLB	19	1.77	5.86	6.80	-0.7				

San Francisco Giants 2019

Logan Webb RHP
Born: 11/18/96 Age: 22 Bats: R Throws: R
Height: 6'2" Weight: 220 Origin: Round 4, 2014 Draft (#118 overall)

YEAR	TEAM	LVL	AGE	W	L	SV	G	GS	IP	H	HR	BB/9	K/9	K	GB%	BABIP
2016	AUG	A	19	2	3	0	9	9	42	54	7	2.6	6.4	30	57%	.326
2017	SLO	A-	20	2	0	0	15	0	28	26	1	2.2	10.0	31	68%	.325
2018	SJO	A+	21	1	3	0	21	20	74	54	2	4.4	9.0	74	48%	.274
2018	RIC	AA	21	1	2	0	6	6	30²	30	4	3.2	7.6	26	52%	.289
2019	SFN	MLB	22	1	1	0	3	3	15	15	2	3.8	8.0	13	47%	.295

Breakout: 15% Improve: 21% Collapse: 6% Attrition: 13% MLB: 30%
Comparables: Greg Reynolds, Jonathan Pettibone, Paul Blackburn

Seventeen-year-olds who can chuck it 96 mph don't grow on trees, so when Webb lit up scouts' guns six weeks before the 2014 draft, he went from an anonymous high-schooler bound for Cal Poly to a coveted prospect in the blink of an eye. The Giants plucked the country-strong right-hander out of their Central Valley backyard, handed him $600,000, and then watched him flounder in the low minors before undergoing Tommy John surgery. Four years into his career, Webb suddenly popped back onto prospect radars last summer, touching 97 while fearlessly pounding hitters inside. The command and secondary stuff lag behind the plus fastball, as you might expect given Webb's resume, but he has the makings of at least a seventh-inning arm, an outcome that seemed remote not too long ago.

YEAR	TEAM	LVL	AGE	WHIP	ERA	DRA	WARP	MPH	FB%	WHF	CSP
2016	AUG	A	19	1.57	6.21	3.72	0.7				
2017	SLO	A-	20	1.18	2.89	3.10	0.6				
2018	SJO	A+	21	1.22	1.82	6.27	-0.8				
2018	RIC	AA	21	1.34	3.82	3.80	0.5				
2019	SFN	MLB	22	1.41	4.42	4.94	0.0				

Garrett Williams LHP

Born: 09/15/94 Age: 24 Bats: L Throws: L
Height: 6'1" Weight: 200 Origin: Round 7, 2016 Draft (#215 overall)

YEAR	TEAM	LVL	AGE	W	L	SV	G	GS	IP	H	HR	BB/9	K/9	K	GB%	BABIP
2016	GIA	RK	21	1	0	0	3	1	7	4	0	3.9	6.4	5	63%	.211
2016	SLO	A-	21	1	2	0	7	7	25^1	28	1	5.0	7.8	22	59%	.342
2017	AUG	A	22	4	3	0	12	11	64	59	0	3.5	8.2	58	63%	.296
2017	SJO	A+	22	2	2	0	6	5	33	28	3	2.7	10.4	38	58%	.287
2018	RIC	AA	23	3	9	1	33	15	81^2	96	6	6.7	8.0	73	55%	.353
2019	SFN	MLB	24	4	5	0	25	14	76^2	77	8	5.8	7.9	67	50%	.319

Breakout: 7% Improve: 10% Collapse: 4% Attrition: 11% MLB: 17%
Comparables: Ricky Romero, Curtis Partch, Jonny Venters

Yo-yo'd between the rotation and bullpen at Double-A Richmond, Williams never found a groove during the regular season, so the Giants gave the lefty a second chance in the Arizona Fall League. There, Williams showcased the plus fastball and curveball that keep scouts coming despite the poor control and foul body language that turns them off. The former Oklahoma State Cowboy struggles to throw strikes because of a wacky delivery that he can't repeat, and his changeup is two full grades behind his heater and breaker. With two plus offerings, Williams should at least find work as a specialist, and at 24, he's much closer to settling for that floor than he is to reaching his mid-rotation ceiling.

YEAR	TEAM	LVL	AGE	WHIP	ERA	DRA	WARP	MPH	FB%	WHF	CSP
2016	GIA	RK	21	1.00	2.57	3.64	0.1				
2016	SLO	A-	21	1.66	5.68	4.18	0.3				
2017	AUG	A	22	1.31	2.25	3.76	1.1				
2017	SJO	A+	22	1.15	2.45	3.58	0.6				
2018	RIC	AA	23	1.92	6.06	5.22	0.0				
2019	SFN	MLB	24	1.65	4.98	5.79	-0.5				

LINEOUTS

Hitters

HITTER	POS	TEAM	LVL	AGE	PA	R	2B	3B	HR	RBI	BB	K	SB	CS	AVG/OBP/SLG	DRC+	WARP
John Andreoli	RF	SEA	MLB	28	6	0	0	0	0	0	1	2	0	0	.200/.333/.200	68	0.0
	RF	TAC	AAA	28	388	54	18	5	3	36	55	86	19	5	.287/.397/.401	116	1.2
	RF	BAL	MLB	28	61	4	2	0	0	4	4	17	2	0	.232/.279/.268	69	-0.1
Aaron Bond	CF	AUG	A	21	94	12	1	0	0	6	12	29	3	1	.205/.301/.218	73	-0.2
	CF	SLO	A-	21	201	38	6	5	14	39	14	58	8	1	.268/.320/.585	106	0.2
Ryder Jones	4C	SAC	AAA	24	482	57	22	4	11	59	30	106	2	2	.274/.328/.417	91	0.7
	4C	SFN	MLB	24	8	2	0	0	2	3	0	5	0	0	.375/.375/1.125	82	0.0
Rene Rivera	C	ANA	MLB	34	87	8	4	0	4	11	4	32	0	0	.244/.287/.439	75	0.1
	C	ATL	MLB	34	4	0	0	0	0	0	0	3	0	0	.000/.000/.000	72	0.0
Brock Stassi	1B	ROC	AAA	28	133	14	6	0	2	13	15	28	0	1	.211/.316/.316	72	-0.4
	1B	SAC	AAA	28	84	11	10	0	0	11	19	14	0	0	.391/.536/.547	190	0.9
Luis Toribio	3B	DGI	Rk	17	274	44	13	1	10	39	51	62	4	1	.270/.423/.479	157	1.2

As anyone who read Colm Toibin's Brooklyn (or the many, many more people who saw the movie) could tell you: any given AL East roster has room for either Darren Christopher O'Day or **John Francis Andreoli**. Not both. Never both. ⓥ A lithe athlete who looks the part, **Aaron Bond** has the power and speed to be rated AAA someday, but he'll need to smooth his choppy swing path to rise above junk status first. ⓥ **Miguel Gomez** and CB Bucknor share a common understanding of the strike zone, only Gomez's major-league employment actually depends on his professional development. ⓥ Despite logging only eight plate appearances in the majors last season, **Ryder Jones** experienced the Three True Outcomes and a great deal of pain. He homered twice, struck out five times and gave way to a Brandon Belt walk after dislocating his left knee on a swing. ⓥ Signed for $2.6 million last summer, Dominican shortstop **Marco Luciano** has an explosive swing with precocious all-fields power, which gives him a chance to hit in the heart of the order. The athletic teenager may outgrow the six spot, but his offensive tools project favorably even with a move to third base or right field. ⓥ The Braves claimed **Rene Rivera** off waivers when their catchers were momentarily dropping like flies, marking his eighth organization. He's had a nice run as a defense-first depth guy and should soak in what's left of it. ⓥ **Brock Stassi**'s baseball travels took him out to Williamsport and down to Caracas, from the Mexican Pacific Winter League to indy ball in the Atlantic, before a stop with Triple-A Sacramento brought him to within 40 miles of his hometown. The journeyman can resume his odyssey with renewed confidence after a 21-game star turn with the River Cats. ⓥ If you're looking for a diamond in the rough that is the Giants' system, look no further than **Luis Toribio**, whose hitting tools awed DSL scouts last summer. The third baseman will be the main attraction on the complex when he comes stateside this year. ⓛ In the middle of August, the Brewers seemingly could not win a day game, so injured veteran **Stephen Vogt** began delivering day-game lineup cards. Milwaukee reversed fortunes immediately, making Vogt's feat the most interesting way to earn three million bucks.

Pitchers

PITCHER	TEAM	LVL	AGE	W	L	SV	G	GS	IP	H	HR	BB/9	K/9	K	GB%	WHIP	ERA	DRA	WARP
Melvin Adon	SJO	A+	24	2	5	0	16	15	77^2	82	6	3.9	8.2	71	57%	1.49	4.87	5.91	-0.5
Jamie Callahan	LVG	AAA	23	0	1	1	7	0	8^1	14	0	4.3	9.7	9	45%	2.16	9.72	8.15	-0.3
Juan De Paula	STA	A-	20	2	2	0	10	9	47^1	35	1	4.9	8.7	46	46%	1.29	1.71	5.84	-0.4
Trevor Gott	WAS	MLB	25	0	2	0	20	0	19	19	4	4.7	7.1	15	58%	1.53	5.68	6.11	-0.3
	SYR	AAA	25	1	1	3	28	0	29^1	23	1	2.5	11.7	38	56%	1.06	3.68	3.13	0.7
Tyler Herb	GIA	Rk	26	1	1	0	4	4	12^2	13	0	2.8	5.7	8	50%	1.34	5.68	3.75	0.3
	SAC	AAA	26	2	8	0	13	13	70^2	85	9	3.6	7.5	59	39%	1.60	5.35	4.53	0.8
Chase Johnson	RIC	AA	26	2	5	0	18	18	58^1	52	3	3.2	5.7	37	55%	1.25	3.86	4.21	0.8
Derek Law	SFN	MLB	27	1	0	0	7	0	13^1	16	2	5.4	8.1	12	42%	1.80	7.43	3.72	0.2
	SAC	AAA	27	1	3	8	33	0	40^2	34	2	2.0	9.5	43	49%	1.06	4.20	2.61	1.2
Jose Lopez	LOU	AAA	24	5	13	0	26	26	141	142	19	2.6	7.5	117	31%	1.30	4.47	6.73	-1.9
Steven Okert	SAC	AAA	26	2	1	1	33	0	31^2	37	3	2.3	12.2	43	29%	1.42	4.55	3.16	0.7
	SFN	MLB	26	0	0	0	10	0	7^1	4	1	0.0	9.8	8	42%	0.55	1.23	2.89	0.2
Tyler Rogers	SAC	AAA	27	3	2	3	51	0	67^2	50	4	3.1	8.0	60	62%	1.08	2.13	3.41	1.3
Patrick Ruotolo	SJO	A+	23	3	0	6	14	0	18^1	12	0	3.4	12.8	26	40%	1.04	1.47	3.46	0.3
	RIC	AA	23	1	1	4	23	0	26	18	5	3.5	12.5	36	31%	1.08	2.42	2.95	0.6
Pat Venditte	OKL	AAA	33	4	2	4	45	0	51^1	30	1	2.5	10.9	62	44%	0.86	1.75	2.78	1.4
	LAN	MLB	33	0	0	0	15	0	14	11	1	1.9	5.8	9	40%	1.00	2.57	3.15	0.3
Jake Wong	SLO	A-	21	0	2	0	11	11	27^1	28	1	2.0	8.9	27	53%	1.24	2.30	4.26	0.3

An all-gas thrower for most of his career, **Melvin Adon** opened eyes in the Arizona Fall League with a sharp slider and improved control. He'll work the late innings in short order if those gains hold up. ⓛ **Jamie Callahan** didn't make the Mets' bullpen out of Spring Training and got off to a brutal start in Vegas, but when you're a Mets pitcher, things can always get worse. He went under the knife for shoulder surgery in June and missed the rest of the season. ⓛ Acquired from the Yankees in the Andrew McCutchen trade, **Juan De Paula** flashes three above-average pitches and has ample velocity projection, making him a potential riser on prospect lists as he matures. ⓛ Issuing a correction on a previous Lineout of ours, regarding the Nationals bullpen. You should not, under any circumstances, add **Trevor Gott** to it. ⓛ **Jandel Gustave** spent the season recovering from Tommy John and will spend the offseason looking for work, having elected free agency. Recovering his command might take a while, but he's a worthwhile project for some team. ⓧ Among the many inconveniences of shuttling between Triple-A and the majors, potential up-and-down arm **Tyler Herb** would need to have two barbers on call to maintain his flow. ⓧ Perhaps the most anonymous 40-man roster member in the league, **Chase Johnson** has held the distinction since November of 2016 without anyone noticing. He has a plus fastball and solid changeup, but doesn't miss enough bats. ⓧ A former top-100 prospect, **Pierce Johnson** still has the dandy curveball that earned him that status, but shoddy fastball command keeps him from leveraging his bender into a stable big-league role. He'll spend 2019 in Japan. ⓧ **Casey Kelly** never lived up to his first-round draft position, but last year, he got to start a major-league game with his dad bench-coaching in the other dugout. That's a cooler experience than many of his highly touted peers will ever enjoy. ⓧ With the right-hander's career in a tailspin since 2017, it seems the Trump administration is a real threat to the rule of **Derek Law**. ⓧ While Reds pitchers were giving up homers at an incredible rate, **Jose Lopez** decided to get in on the action and make sure he fit in once he was given a shot at doing the same. He gave up nearly as many dingers in 2018 as he did in his entire pro career beforehand, and we'll see if that strategy of imitation pays off. ⓧ Buried on the depth chart by veteran imports, **Steven Okert** still has the slider and deception to reemerge as a useful specialist. ⓧ **Tyler Rogers** doesn't throw as hard as fellow submariners Brad Ziegler and Darren O'Day, but he's shaved his walk rate over three tours in Triple-A and might have novelty value as a specialist. ⓧ Stocky right-hander **Patrick Ruotolo** uses a deceptive motion to play up his solid-average fastball and curve. He's trending toward a late-inning role with a 37 percent strikeout rate through two-plus seasons in the minors. ⓧ **Jose Valdez** owns a high-90s fastball, a tight slider and the highest HR/9 rate of any Modern Era pitcher with at least 50 career innings in the major leagues. ⓧ Ambidextrous marvel **Pat Venditte** has proven that he's probably overqualified for Triple-A, but his offerings haven't yet translated to sustained, big-league success. That last sentence also reads the same from right to left as from left to right. Just kidding. That would've been cool, though. ⓧ Third-rounder **Jake Wong** ran his fastball up to 97 as a Cape Cod League reliever, but with a handful of average to solid offerings, the Grand Canyon University product deserves a fair chance to start.

Giants Prospects

The State of the System:
Joey Bart and Heliot Ramos are really cool. Past that, it's a Giants prospect list.

The Top Ten:

1. Joey Bart C
OFP: 60   Likely: 55   ETA: Late 2020
Born: 12/15/96   Age: 22   Bats: R   Throws: R   Height: 6'3"   Weight: 220
Origin: Round 1, 2018 Draft (#2 overall)

The Report: Bart shot up 2018 draft boards on the back of his improving defense. He's a good catch-and-throw guy with a plus arm and he's athletic behind the plate. His receiving is a bit of a work in progress—he can get a little boxy—but should end up at least average. I believe as a prospect writer that I am also contractually obligated to mention that he called his own games in college.

While he's likely to be a solid hand defensively, the real reason Bart went second overall—and had occasional 1.1 scuttlebutt—is the potential with the bat. Only four catchers in 2018 posted an .800 OPS, and Bart has that kind of offensive upside due to his combination of plus bat speed and plus raw. He can still get front-footed on offspeed stuff and the swing can get long in the zone, so there is some hit tool risk that may limit the upside in the profile. But the bar for catcher offense is so low that even a .250, 15-20 HR profile would make him a solid everyday option behind the dish.

The Risks: Medium. His pro debut went extremely well, but an ACC bat mashing in the Northwest League is hardly shocking. There are the usual developmental risks for a prospect who hasn't even seen full-season ball yet, but the glove gives him a strong starting base. Remember though, catchers are weird.

Ben Carsley's Fantasy Take: Catching prospects are the football, reality is Lucy and I am Charlie Brown, but this time I'm just not gonna try to kick the field goal. Bart could very well emerge as a top-10 fantasy backstop capable of putting up 20 bombs a season with a tolerable average. But when do you feel comfortable guessing he'll emerge as that dude? It probably won't happen right when he reaches the major leagues, if the typical learning curve for catchers tells us anything. And again, the upside here is good but not great—we're not talking about a prime Gary Sanchez-type fantasy talent. It's not Bart's fault that he isn't a top-101 prospect, but he's still not. If you really love this profile, go grab Danny Jansen or something. At least he's closer.

San Francisco Giants 2019

2 **Heliot Ramos   OF**   OFP: 60   Likely: 50   ETA: 2021
Born: 09/07/99   Age: 19   Bats: R   Throws: R   Height: 6'2"   Weight: 185
Origin: Round 1, 2017 Draft (#19 overall)

The Report: After getting drafted 17th overall in 2017 and signing for $3.1 million, Ramos was the talk of the Giants system last year. An up-and-down initial full-season taste in 2018 tempered some of the excitement and revealed a raw prospect. The big question is how much he'll hit. He shows some feel for using all fields and he barrels the ball consistently when he sees it well, but he's overly aggressive at times and susceptible to basic sequencing. He doesn't turn on the ball enough to utilize his above-average-potential power yet and is more of a gap hitter now. Physically, he's essentially maxed out.

His run tool didn't show up in A-ball as expected: He was average at best down the line, and he'll only get slower. He has the arm for any outfield spot and reads the ball well for his age. Evaluators also wonder whether he'll have the range for center as he gets older (one scout even suggested a move to second base down the road). There are a lot of questions about his ultimate future, but Ramos has the tools to be a major-leaguer, perhaps as more of an average regular than any kind of star.

The Risks: High. Ramos is still getting his feet wet in pro ball, and a full-season assignment unmasked some areas that need improving. He has the tools to be a major-leaguer but also a long way to go before they can actualize. He needs to hit and tap into his power potential.

Ben Carsley's Fantasy Take: Well… at least 2018 has conditioned us to be used to disappointment. Ramos was a BP Fantasy Team favorite heading into last season, so that's a pretty rough report to read all around. He'll still be a top-101 guy because I'm stubborn and there are some loud fantasy tools that remain, but for the time being it seems prudent to knock Ramos down several pegs. Just what this farm system needed…

3 **Shaun Anderson   RHP**   OFP: 55   Likely: 50   ETA: 2019
Born: 10/29/94   Age: 24   Bats: R   Throws: R   Height: 6'4"   Weight: 225
Origin: Round 3, 2016 Draft (#88 overall)

The Report: This may seem a little bit early to be hitting the polished, older, four-average pitches starter, but this is also the Giants list, so we are running right about on time. Acquired in the Eduardo Nunez deal last Summer, Anderson has actually been a nice development story as a converted starter. You know the dossier by now. It's an average fastball that he can run up to 95 at times, a potentially above-average slider, and improving changeup that gives him an armside option against lefties, and a "fourth pitch," in this case a fringy curve. Add in a frame built to log innings and you've got yourself a fourth starter stew going. The last step for Anderson is to refine his command enough to walk the tightrope against major league hitters. And if Giants Devil Magic exists (light some patchouli), Anderson seems as good a candidate for the Dereck Rodriguez Memorial confusing sub-3.00 ERA season as anyone in the system.

The Risks: Low? Medium? Can I say Smedium? It's not overpowering stuff, it's less command than you'd like with less than overpowering stuff, but he's also just about ready.

Ben Carsley's Fantasy Take: Borrrrrrrrrrrrinnnnnnnnnng. Anderson may be of interest in deep leagues as a spot starter, but that's about it. Thank god we have seven of these guys to go : (

4 Alexander Canario   OF   OFP: 60   Likely: 45   ETA: 2023
Born: 05/07/00   Age: 19   Bats: R   Throws: R   Height: 6'1"   Weight: 165
Origin: International Free Agent, 2016

The Report: We started hearing about what a steal the Giants got with Canario when he made his pro debut in the 2017 DSL. That chatter got a lot louder with his 2018 debut stateside. This is a lot of tools and projectability for five figures—a chance at all of them, really. He's got a quick bat, a big swing, and a body that projects out to give him a chance to hit the ball far with that quick bat and big swing. He's athletic, he runs well, and he has a shot to stay in center. It's potentially a big profile.

We don't yet know if he can identify and hit good pitching. He's yet to graduate out of the complex leagues, and as you'll see us point out every now and again, the complex leagues frankly more closely resemble "practice" than "organized baseball." There's some drift and bat wrap in his swing. We've also seen enough big swings on projectable bodies that *didn't* grow into them to be slightly cautious. A likely assignment somewhere between rookie ball and Low-A will be quite telling here, both in how aggressively he's moved and how he handles it.

The Risks: Extreme. He's a complex-league bat and he's going to need to make good on a lot of projection. He could be the best prospect in this system at some point fairly soon, or this could be his high water mark.

Ben Carsley's Fantasy Take: If you're looking to gamble on a high-upside talent that not a ton of people in dynasty circles are super hip to yet, Canario is a solid choice. This will be a slow burn, but once guys like this click they tend to jump into the middle of the top-101 pretty quickly. Also, if you're just here for the fantasy takes, you can pretty much stop reading now.

5 Logan Webb   RHP   OFP: 55   Likely: 45   ETA: 2020
Born: 11/18/96   Age: 22   Bats: R   Throws: R   Height: 6'2"   Weight: 220
Origin: Round 4, 2014 Draft (#118 overall)

The Report: The Giants bought Webb out of a college commitment back in 2014, but after a nondescript first season he lost big chunks of 2016 and 2017 to Tommy John surgery and subsequent rehab. Last year, he returned to log 20 tightly-guarded starts at San Jose and a half-dozen more in Double-A. The stuff returned with a vengeance, and it is some of the system's best: a riding heater that touches 97 with life in the zone, a low-80s slider that teases two-plane action with solid bite, and a developing mid-80s change that flashes average tumble and fade. He's big and thick, yet athletic and he repeats his balanced delivery with reasonable consistency.

The Risks: High. The Giants have been slow and steady in their rebuilding of Webb after Tommy John, only elevating him to the 80-plus pitch range in his final seven starts of the season. The drive can get inconsistent and there's a bit of effort to the delivery that can joggle his command out of whack. The changeup lags at present, and all of these nicks combined with the red-flag medicals is enough to introduce significant bullpen risk.

Ben Carsley's Fantasy Take: Do you wish Shaun Anderson was worse?

6. Sean Hjelle   RHP   OFP: 55   Likely: 45   ETA: 2021
Born: 05/07/97   Age: 22   Bats: R   Throws: R   Height: 6'11"   Weight: 225
Origin: Round 2, 2018 Draft (#45 overall)

The Report: If Hjelle makes the majors, he will tie Jon Rauch for tallest pitcher in major league history, and he's got a pretty good shot to do that (Philadelphia's Kyle Young may beat him there, though). Despite his long and lean frame, Hjelle has a relatively simple, compact (again—relatively) delivery that he repeats well. He throws strikes, working off a sinking low-90s fastball. His breaker can get a bit slurvy at times, but it flashes as an above-average, tight downer curve around 80. The change is fringy at present, as they so often are. Hjelle's height is gonna create weird angles for hitters, and he's already a very polished arm. If the secondaries don't get all the way there, he has a reasonable fallback profile as… well, it might look a lot like Jon Rauch.

The Risks: High. Limited pro track record, needs further refinement of his secondaries.

Ben Carsley's Fantasy Take: Gun to your head you should probably take Hjelle above Anderson or Webb in fantasy, but why on earth is someone forcing you to draft a guy from the Giants top-10 list?

7. Heath Quinn   OF   OFP: 50   Likely: 45   ETA: 2020
Born: 06/07/95   Age: 24   Bats: R   Throws: R   Height: 6'3"   Weight: 220
Origin: Round 3, 2016 Draft (#95 overall)

The Report: 2017 was a lost year for the former third-rounder, as Quinn missed the season's first month recovering from the dreaded broken hamate, then lost a bunch *more* time battling a just-as-dreaded shoulder injury. He wasn't exactly a picture of health again this past season either, but it was a Ripken-esque performance, relatively speaking. And when he was on the field, the big-time raw power that got him drafted resurfaced at High-A. It's an easy plus tool, if not better, and he shows a baseline of plate discipline that helped him bring more of it into games. He's got average wheels for now, along with an above-average arm that should hold serve in right.

The Risks: High. Quinn's medical file is as big as the outfield at AT&T Park. There's enough athleticism and agility that the defensive value should be at least a marginal net positive, but at its core this is a right-handed, bat-first corner profile. Everything needs to click for him to hold a significant role.

Ben Carsley's Fantasy Take: Between the injury history, the future home ballpark, and the modest upside it's tough to get very excited about Quinn. Could he hold some value if he manages to earn an everyday spot? Sure. But he's the type of guy teams are always trying to improve on, and odds are he'll spend as much time on your DL as in your active lineup. Reserve for only the deepest of leagues.

8. Tyler Beede   RHP

OFP: 50   Likely: 40   ETA: Debuted in 2018
Born: 05/23/93   Age: 26   Bats: R   Throws: R   Height: 6'3"   Weight: 211
Origin: Round 1, 2014 Draft (#14 overall)

The Report: I started writing about prospects in an official, extremely online capacity in 2011. That summer I popped onto an old internet friend's now defunct pro wrestling podcast (Hola, TH). We happened to record late at night, right after the signing deadline for that year's draft. As we sort of tap danced at the open to the pod, I mentioned that I was up to follow late-breaking draft stuff and the only major draftee who hadn't signed was Tyler Beede, who was popped late in the first round by Toronto. We chatted about the value of a Vanderbilt education, and what the best-case scenario might be for him in three years before launching into a discussion of God knows what, probably Dragon Gate Pro Wrestling. Anyway, this is all to say there is prospect fatigue… and then there is Tyler Beede.

The long and winding road deposited Beede as a spot starter in the Giants rotation in April. It didn't go great. The profile hasn't changed, well, ever really. A low-90s fastball with good two-seam action that he doesn't always command. A four-seamer that'll touch 95. A decent cutter, a change-up that flashes above-average now, a show-me curve. The Giants tried him in the pen back in Sacramento; the stuff didn't really pop, the cutter rounded off and was sliderish, and he still doesn't throw enough strikes or miss as many bats as you (and two different orgs now) would have thought. He's going to age out of the Selective Service soon. TH has two kids now. Dragon Gate is in the midst of a tumultuous transitionary period, it's future uncertain. I'm still thinking (and writing) about Tyler Beede.

The Risks: Low, I guess. I don't feel good about it. I don't feel good about any of this.

Ben Carsley's Fantasy Take: Odds are whatever name value Beede once had doesn't count for much in your league, but if you play with guys and gals who stopped paying attention like three years ago, it couldn't hurt to float Beede's name. Then again, why do you still own Beede?

9. Aramis Garcia C
OFP: 50 Likely: 40 ETA: Debuted in 2018
Born: 01/12/93 Age: 26 Bats: R Throws: R Height: 6'2" Weight: 220
Origin: Round 2, 2014 Draft (#52 overall)

The Report: Look, I don't mean to be pithy or cruel or even sardonic, and I'm (arguably too) often sardonic. Giants fans deserve the same effort as every other team… but Garcia's a backup catcher. That Double-A line reads like a dictionary definition backup catcher. There are only 60 jobs, man. Well, maybe more when Joe Maddon gets a little weird, or somebody, usually Ned Yost I'd guess, wants to carry three catchers.

Garcia will put on the gear and give a decent accounting of himself. He's improved to averagish behind the plate. He'll give you sub-2.0 times on your Accusplit, for all that matters nowadays. His game-calling and receiving have improved enough. At the plate, he'll run into a few, due to his plus raw and loft. He doesn't have Drew Butera's hair or Anthony Recker's ass, but the Royal Fraternity of backup catchers only asks that you have below-average offensive tools. Anything else is a bonus when your poor prospect writer is trying to fill 150 words or so, let alone the poor sucker who has to write the fantasy blurb here.

The Risks: Low. Voros's Law applies to his major league cameo, but it was a major league cameo. The main risk is he gets squeezed out in a catching-rich org, but these rankings happen in a vacuum.

Ben Carsley's Fantasy Take: The Larry David unsure Curb Your Enthusiasm gif, but only the first part where he looks wildly uncomfortable before reconsidering.

10. Chris Shaw 1B
OFP: 50 Likely: 40 ETA: Debuted in 2018
Born: 10/20/93 Age: 25 Bats: L Throws: R Height: 6'3" Weight: 226
Origin: Round 1, 2015 Draft (#31 overall)

The Report: Shaw's strikeout issues became a real problem for him in 2018 despite mashing in the PCL. He has a yoked-up, uppercut swing that allows him to tap into his plus raw power, but it leaves him very vulnerable to stuff moving down or away from him. The bat speed is only average so he has to make decisions quickly, and the decision was rarely to take a pitch, as his walk rate continued to erode. You can manage this profile as a Three True Outcomes slugger, but considering that he's blocked by Brandon Belt at first and a below-average defender in a corner outfield spot, a slugging-heavy .800 OPS isn't that attractive, even if you directly import his Triple-A line. Of course, that's not how baseball works, and major league arms abused Shaw at times in his first taste of the show. All is not lost of course, and he has a long track record of production—and the aforementioned raw power—but the clock starts ticking quickly for corner bat prospects who struggle in the bigs.

The Risks: Medium. So, phrasing risks for these types of profiles is difficult. The actual risk is that he doesn't hit enough and passes into the Quad-A realm that has claimed so many TTO corner mashers before. Even if he does hit pretty close to the projection, you are always looking to upgrade from a Role 5 corner bat.

Ben Carsley's Fantasy Take: *takes deep breath* There's a pretty solid argument to be made that Shaw is the fourth-best fantasy prospect in this system. That does not make him good of course, but we've seen lots of guys with this profile hold short-term value before. We've also seen lots of them tank. Aren't you glad we're done with this system?

Others of note:

Jalen Miller, IF, High-A San Jose

We've been calling Miller a project at the plate since he was drafted, and the Giants finally started to see some deliverables in 2018. We're not ready to declare a minimal viable product here yet; Miller is still hyper-aggressive at the plate. But he had enough hand-eye and bat speed to make it work across a second pass of the Cal League at least. He's an above-average runner and has settled in as a solid defender at second base. The likely range of outcomes here still runs from "good utility player" to "up-and-down utility player," but we'll just roll everything else over into our 2019 Q1 goals.

Jake Wong, RHP

Wong—the Giants third round pick—isn't all that different from Sean Hjelle, minus, oh, nine inches or so. He can pop 95 once in a while with some riding life up, but works more low-90s and the heater can be a bit true. His breaking ball vacillates between a humpy, downer curve that he can change eye levels with, and a tighter backfoot slider option with more gloveside action. These may be two separate pitches but they tend to bleed together a bit, and the middle ground can get slurvy. His changeup is even less of a factor than Hjelle's, and there's more effort in the delivery. The frame looks like a starter's but given the state of the current arsenal, he might be better teasing out a consistent breaking ball he likes and letting it loose in relief.

Mac Marshall, LHP

"The stuff's not that far off Logan Webb" was a thing written in our internal discussion of Marshall w/r/t the Giants list. The health/durability concerns are dead even though, as Marshall was weaned back onto the mound slowly following 2017 elbow surgery. He's never thrown more than 67 innings in a pro season, so as intriguing as the low 90s fastball/high 80s cutter combination is from the left side, you have to wonder if he can hold up under a starter's workload. The third pitch is there, assuming the feel for his potential plus change returns. Marshall might be best off working multi-inning relief where perhaps the fastball will tick up and he can eschew his below-average slider. But we'd like to see a full healthy season before we rank him "not that far off Logan Webb."

Jacob Gonzalez, 3B, Low-A Agusta

Son of Luis, Jacob Gonzalez carries himself on and off the field like a person who has been around a locker room his entire life, which he has. He's a positive clubhouse guy and someone you want in your organization as a person. He also has a tireless work ethic and puts a lot into his defense. It might not keep him at third base long-term, however, because his actions and arm aren't suited for the position. If he moves to left field, he has to max out his hit profile. The bat is quick and he can tap into his above-average power. He's aggressive at the plate and has some swing-and-miss, but the stick is major-league quality, and he might have a future as a bench bat.

Top Talents 25 and Under (born 4/1/93 or later):

1. Joey Bart
2. Heliot Ramos
3. Shaun Anderson
4. Steven Duggar
5. Alexander Canario
6. Logan Webb
7. Sean Hjelle
8. Heath Quinn
9. Tyler Beede
10. Aramis Garcia

Uh… hello? Is this thing on?

We all have our strengths and weaknesses in life, and while building a club capable of peeling off three championships in five years was a strength of Brian Sabean's, integrating the next wave of young players to extend that contention window proved… challenging.

Duggar dipped his toes into big league waters for the first time last season and they were warm enough, before yet another injury—this time a dislocated shoulder—ended his season prematurely. At his healthy best, Duggar will battle through at-bats, take some walks, ambush mistakes, and do a reasonable job covering San Francisco's cavernous centerfield. He should open 2019 with a shot to start in center.

Beyond him, what you see in our prospect list is what you get. You could make a case for Ryder Jones to sneak onto this list at the back, given Beede and Garcia's stagnation. But a return engagement at Sacramento last year didn't go nearly as swimmingly as his first crack, and it was the Panda's Geriatric Belly that got the corner reps when injuries opened up a job, not the young buck. Reyes Moronta has aged out of consideration, and it's a field full of crickets after that.

A new regime and what should be a string of high draft picks over the next couple seasons offers potential for a relatively quick infusion of new blood into these ranks going forward, but given the state of the franchise at present, it feels likely to get darker before that light shines in.

Part 3: Featured Articles

The Hole in The Shift is Fixing Itself

Russell Carleton

I've been on a bit of a mission against The Shift of late. I'm not out to get The Shift for the usual reasons that people oppose it. The words "the right way to play the game" won't be found on my lips. If a team wants to pursue a strategy that is within the rules and it works, then by all means, they have my blessing (not that they need it). Instead, my concern with The Shift is a worry that it doesn't work, or at least that it has a flaw that needs fixing.

The data show that while The Shift does a decent job of preventing singles on balls in play (what it's supposed to do), it also increases the number of walks that happen in front of it, and the number of additional walks outweighs the number of singles saved. It's a problem because you can't throw a guy out if he gets to walk to first base.

But the "why" was important. It seemed that The Shift was changing the way in which pitchers pitched. We saw that there were fewer fastballs thrown in front of The Shift than we might otherwise expect, and that pitchers tended to stay out of the strike zone a little more. Not by a lot. In fact, it might not even be visible to the naked eye. The percentage of pitches that are out of the zone goes from 51.0 to 53.3 from a standard defense (two right/two left) to a full shift (three on one side). That difference stands up even after we control for the types of hitters that get shifted against. And it's enough to drive up the walk rate to where it cancels out the benefits that teams thought they were getting with The Shift… and then some.

But there was some hope. I found that when individual pitchers stayed closer to the in-zone/out-of-zone mix that they used without The Shift on, they could still get the benefits of The Shift without the walk problems. So, in theory, a team could simply figure out a way to convince its pitchers to not fall prey to the walk trap and The Shift would once again be their friend.

It's reasonable to think that some teams might be more hip to this idea than others. Maybe some figured it out a year before the others. Maybe they were better at getting the message across to their pitchers. Or, maybe no one has figured it out yet.

Warning! Gory Mathematical Details Ahead!

I used data from 2015-2017, made available through MLB's data portal, Baseball Savant. They are kind enough to note when teams are using an infield shift (three fielders on one side of second base), as opposed to a "strategic shift" (someone's playing a bit out of position, but it's not quite that drastic) or a "standard" alignment.

Since we're doing this by team, I can't just look at raw walk rates, because we know that some teams have good pitchers and others have not-so-good pitchers. Some have a mix of both. I used the log-odds ratio method to take into account a batter's general walking proclivities, and a pitcher's as well, and then shoving them into a binary logistic regression. Then, I asked the computer to generate a specific coefficient for each team's pitchers, for when they went into The Shift and how that affected their walk rate.

Using those coefficients, I was able to project what would happen if a league-average pitcher faced a league-average hitter (which we expect would product a league-average walk rate; from 2015-2017, 7.7 percent of plate appearances ended in a walk) and then just switched his hat. Here's the top five and the bottom five:

Top 5 Teams	Projected Shift Walk Rate	Bottom 5 Teams	Projected Shift Walk Rate
Rockies	6.2%	Rangers	11.2%
Pirates	6.7%	Mets	10.4%
Indians	7.2%	Dodgers	10.2%
Astros	7.3%	Cardinals	9.9%
Braves	7.7%	Tigers	9.7%

There are probably people out there right now trying to figure out what the common thread is among the top and bottom teams. I'm sure, because this is Baseball Prospectus, people are already trying to make the case that sabermetric "early adopters" have some sort of edge here. I think that the more interesting piece is that by the time you get to fifth place in The Shift, we're at league average.

As a sanity check, I examined the issue on a pitch-by-pitch level, looking at how often pitchers threw their pitches in the GameDay strike zone, and again using the same basic methodology and getting team-specific coefficients. The names on the list re-arranged themselves, but the idea was the same, and the two lists correlated with an R of .593.

There's a reason that I don't usually do this type of leaderboard post. I don't really know what the Rockies, Pirates, Indians, Astros, and Braves have in common, or what they have that the bottom five don't. I can put a shrug emoji here and say, "Well, it must be something!" but that seems like a cop-out. Instead, I'd like to present another table and suggest that the table above doesn't even really matter anymore.

Year	League Percent Outside K Zone (Full Shift)	League Percent in K Zone (No Shift)	Difference
2015	54.1%	51.1%	3.0%
2016	53.3%	50.9%	2.4%
2017	52.6%	50.9%	1.7%
2018	52.0%	50.7%	1.3%

The hole in The Shift is fixing itself, and it's coming down really fast league wide. In my earlier work on The Shift, I suggested that until teams stopped having such a huge difference between their out-of-zone rate with and without The Shift on, there would just be too many walks for The Shift to make sense. It seems that all 30 of them have been working toward just that. I once estimated that it takes about 10 years for an idea to filter its way through baseball. At this rate, it looks like teams are going to catch up a lot faster than that. And yeah, they're all saber-smart now.

It's likely that whatever magic it was that the Rockies and Pirates had has made its way to Texas and Queens. Or is at least on its way. And if teams are committing to fixing the walk problem, then it's likely that they will continue shifting and shifting a lot.

And eventually it's going to actually make sense for them to do it.

—Russell Carleton is a former author of Baseball Prospectus and now an analyst for the New York Mets.

The State of the Quality Start

Rob Mains

One of the seven things you (probably) didn't know about the 2018 season is that quality starts—defined as a start lasting six or more innings with three or fewer earned runs allowed—as a percentage of total starts cratered to an all-time low of 41 percent. I want to look a little more deeply into this, since it's been a while (May of 2016, to be exact) since I've examined quality starts.

The term *quality start* is credited to *Philadelphia Inquirer* sportswriter John Lowe. It's been derided ever since he coined it in December of 1985. Three runs in six innings? That's a 4.50 ERA! In what world is that a measure of quality?

Let's start with that criticism. It's true that 3 x 9 / 6 = 4.5. (You came here for this sort of high-level math, right?) But it's also true that type of start, meeting the bare minimum for earning a quality start, is unusual. Here's the proportion of quality starts in which the pitcher lasted exactly six innings and yielded exactly three earned runs. (I'm going to confine this analysis to the 30-team era, 1998-present. Almost all data retrieved in this article is via the Baseball-Reference Play Index.)

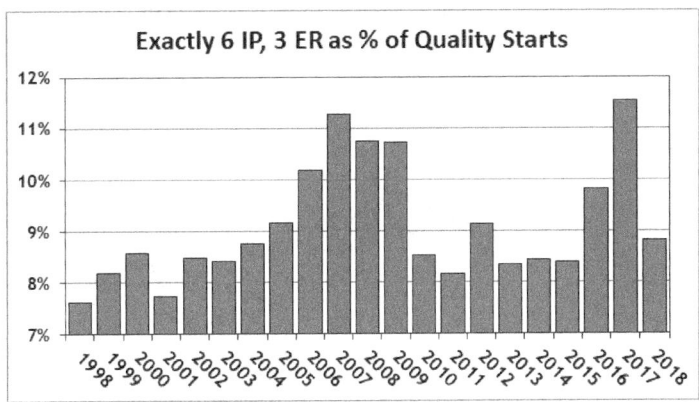

There were 1,997 quality starts in 2018. Only 176, or fewer than one in 11, featured a pitcher going six innings and allowing three earned runs. Put another way, the percentage of quality starts that resulted in a 4.50 ERA (8.8 percent) is less than half the percentage of games in which a batter hit two home runs and his team lost (22.5 percent; 237-69 won-lost). That doesn't impugn hitting two homers.

So if a 4.50 ERA isn't the norm, what is? How good are quality starts?

Pretty good, it turns out. First, on a team level:

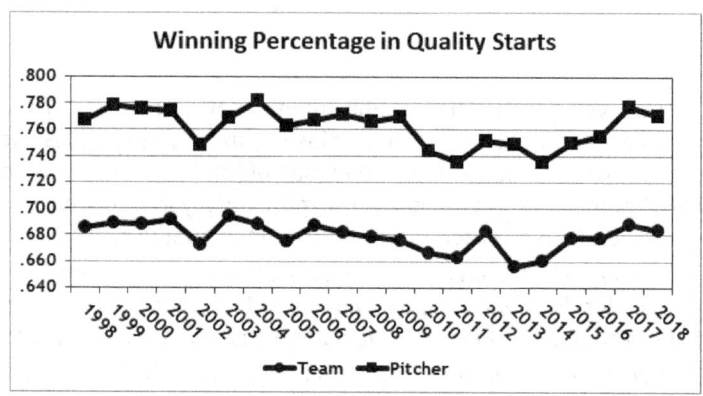

Teams receiving a quality start from their pitcher won 68.4 percent of their games in 2018, in line with the 30-team era average of 67.9 percent. A team with a .684 winning percentage wins 111 games. Getting a quality start is definitely a good thing. Individual pitchers throwing quality starts have a higher winning percentage because a big slice of team losses is assigned to a reliever.

If teams do well in quality starts, how well do the starting pitchers do? Again, very well.

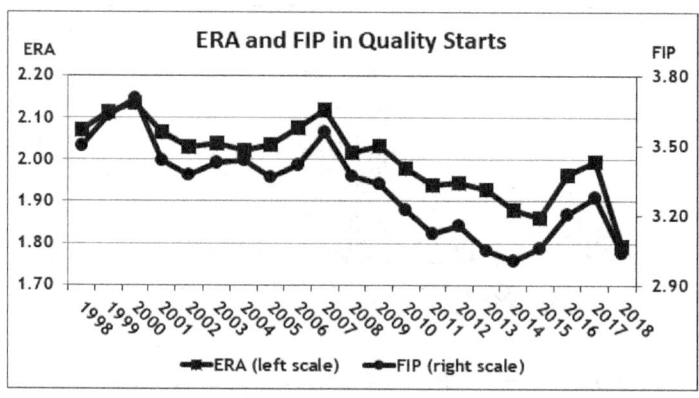

Pitchers in quality starts had a 1.79 ERA (blue line) in 2018, *the lowest in the 30-team era*. Their FIP was higher, 3.04, but still excellent. In the 30-team era, only 2014 had a lower FIP for quality starts, 3.01.

But, of course, the run environment in 2014 was different. Teams in 2014 scored 4.07 runs per game, the fewest in a non-strike year since 1976. They scored 4.45 runs per game in 2018. So surrendering a 3.04 FIP in 2018 is more impressive than 3.01 in 2014. Accordingly, let's look at ERA and FIP in quality starts relative to league averages.

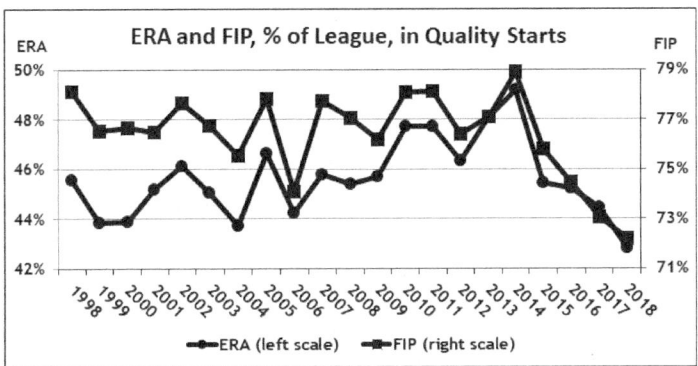

This tells a more dramatic story. Starting pitchers in 2018 gave up a 4.19 ERA and a 4.21 FIP. Starters in quality starts gave up a 1.79 ERA, 43 percent of the league average. Starters in quality starts gave up a 3.04 FIP, 72 percent of the league average. Both of these marks represent lows in the 30-team era.

The takeaway here is this: *Quality starts are better, relative to other starts, than they've ever been over the past 21 years.*

Maybe during the winter I'll look at this over a longer arc of time. For now, though, we can definitively say quality starts are the best they've ever been since the Diamondbacks and Rays joined the majors.

Yet, paradoxically, they're down.

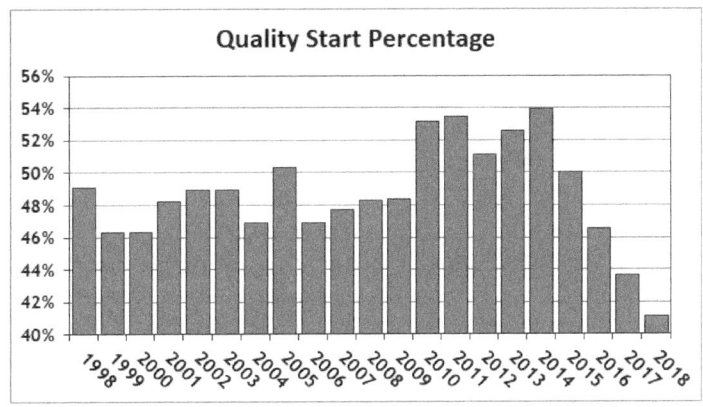

This graph covers only the 30-team era. In my article last week, though, I looked at the years 1908-2018. The result was the same. The 41 percent of starts in 2018 that were quality starts are an all-time low, well below the runners-up: 1930's 43 percent (the year teams scored an all-time record 5.55 runs per game) and last year's 44 percent.

The normal explanation for a dip in quality start percentage is an increase in scoring. When teams score a lot of runs, it's harder for starting pitchers to last six or more innings and limit opponents to three earned runs. From 1998 to 2014, the correlation between runs scored per game and the percentage of starts that were quality starts was -0.94. That means there was an extremely close relationship: More runs, fewer quality starts. Too small a sample? Go back to the start of the Expansion Era, 1961, and the relationship is even more negative, a -0.95 correlation, though 2014.

But that's broken down over the past four years:

- 2015: Runs per game increased from 4.07 to 4.25, quality start percentage decreased from 54.0 to 50.1. Yes, that's a negative relationship, but the regression model would predict a decline of 1.5 percentage points. We got 3.9 instead.
- 2016: Runs per game increased from 4.25 to 4.48, quality start percentage decreased from 50.1 to 46.6. Past experience would suggest a decline of just 1.8 percentage points. We got 3.4.
- 2017: Runs per game increased from 4.48 to 4.65, quality start percentage decreased from 46.6 to 43.6. Again, the direction's right, but the magnitude isn't. Using the relationship from 1998 to 2014, that increase in scoring should've reduced quality starts by 1.3 percentage points, not 2.9.
- 2018: Runs per game declined from 4.65 to 4.45. That should've resulted in the quality start percentage moving in the other direction, rising 1.6 points. It didn't. It fell 2.6 points, as noted, to an all-time low.

Granted, we're talking about just four years here. Maybe they're outliers. But I don't think they are. Quality starts, as noted, are as good or better than ever. But they're rarer than ever as well. And I think I know why.

To get a quality start, you need to allow three or fewer earned and pitch at least six innings. That's 18 outs. Here's a graph showing the number of starting pitchers who limited their opponents to three or fewer earned runs but got pulled after pitching at least five innings but fewer than six:

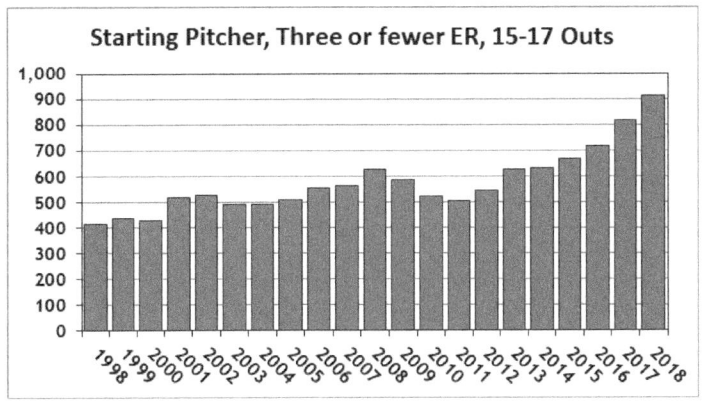

A pitcher getting 15 outs pitched five innings. A pitcher getting 16 outs pitched 5 1/3. A pitcher getting 17 outs pitched 5 2/3. More than ever before, pitchers are being removed from games in which they are within 1-3 outs of a quality start, falling just short of the six-inning finish line. Widespread acknowledgement of the times-through-the-order penalty and a flotilla of available bullpen arms is making the quality start simultaneously both more excellent and more rare.

Which is ironic, given that we saw a new post-war quality start record this season:

Rank	Pitcher	Season	Consecutive QS
1	Jacob deGrom	2018	24
2	Bob Gibson	1968	22
-	Chris Carpenter	2005	22
4	Johan Santana	2004	21
5	Luis Tiant	1968	20
-	Mike Scott	1986	20
-	Jake Arrieta	2015	20
8	Robin Roberts	1952	19
-	Tom Seaver	1973	19
-	Jack Morris	1983	19
-	Greg Maddux	1998	19
-	Josh Johnson	2010	19
-	Jon Lester	2014	19

While there have been longer streaks spread over multiple seasons, no pitcher since World War II threw more consecutive quality starts in one year than Jacob deGrom this year. The fact that he did in a year in which quality starts were the rarest they've ever been adds to the accomplishment.

—*Rob Mains is an author of Baseball Prospectus.*

Heads-Up Hacking—The First Pitch

Matthew Trueblood

Batters fell behind in a higher percentage of all plate appearances in 2018 than in any previous season for which we have pitch-by-pitch data. That kind of granular information goes back only to 1988, but we might safely assume (given all we know about baseball as it had been before that, and as it has been in the years since) that batters have *never* fallen behind at a higher rate than they did last season.

Through the 1990s, the percentage of all plate appearances that began 0-1 hovered in the high 30s and low 40s. In the 2000s, it rose steadily but slowly, through the mid-40s. In 2018, 49.8 percent of all trips to the plate began 0-1. That, as much as anything, captures in microcosm the nature of hitting in MLB today.

A countdown clock toward strike three begins ticking almost the moment a batter takes his place in the box. The league's adjusted OPS+ on the first pitch was higher in 2018 than ever before, and that has been true in most of the last 10 seasons. Batters hit .264/.289/.442 in all plate appearances in which they swung at the first pitch last season, and .241/.330/.395 in all plate appearances in which they took that first offering.

The percentage differences in batting average and isolated power there favor swinging at the first pitch by more than in any season since 1988, while the difference in on-base percentage favors taking by more than ever. If you want to get on base at a decent clip, it's a good idea to be patient, but you run the risk of missing the only chances you'll get to produce power.

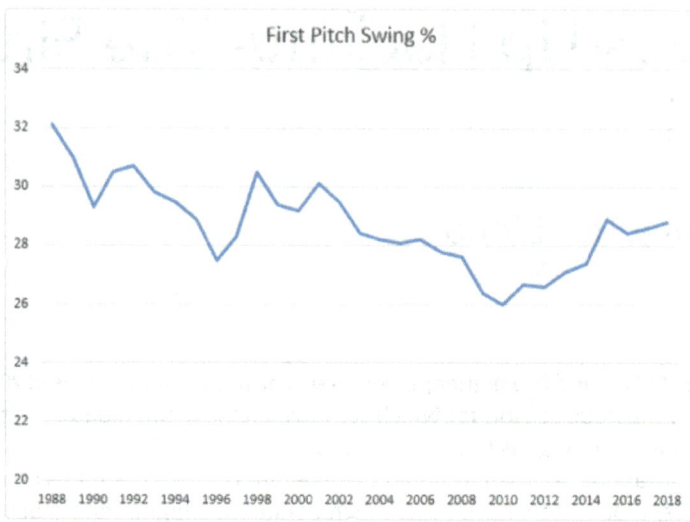

The league swung at the first pitch 28.8 percent of the time in 2018. With the isolated exception of 2015, that's the highest that number has climbed since 2002, but it might not be high enough. With the help of BP research maven Rob McQuown, I looked at the aggregate Called Strike Probability (CSProb) on the first pitch for each season since 2008, when the implementation of PITCHf/x first made measuring that possible. It's risen sharply during that period.

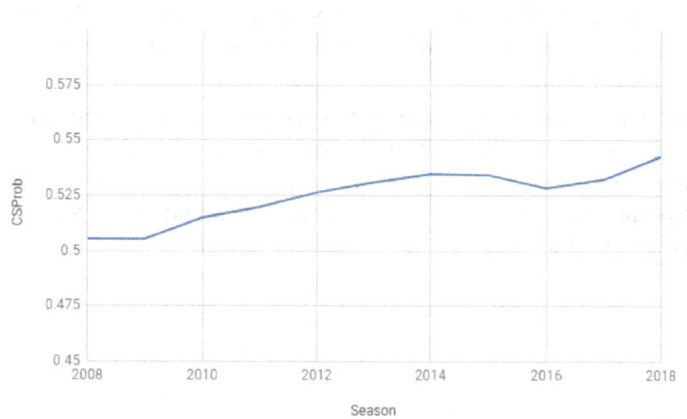

Called Strike Probability, First Pitch of PA (2008-2018)

Called Strike Probability is exactly what it sounds like: a pitch with a given CSProb has roughly that chance of being called a strike, if not swung at. In 2018, a batter who took 100 first pitches from a random sampling of the league's pitchers might expect to fall behind 54 or 55 times—up from 50 or 51 times in 2008. Almost regardless of pitch type (and, notably, especially in the case of fastballs), the first pitch tends to have more of the zone right now than ever before.

Pitchers are better at throwing strikes. They have better stuff, and believe more in their ability to miss bats within the zone. Perhaps most importantly, they know that batters are looking for one thing on the first pitch: a fastball. If they don't get it, they're likely to take the pitch. Check out how the use of sinkers and four-seamers on the first pitch has changed in a decade:

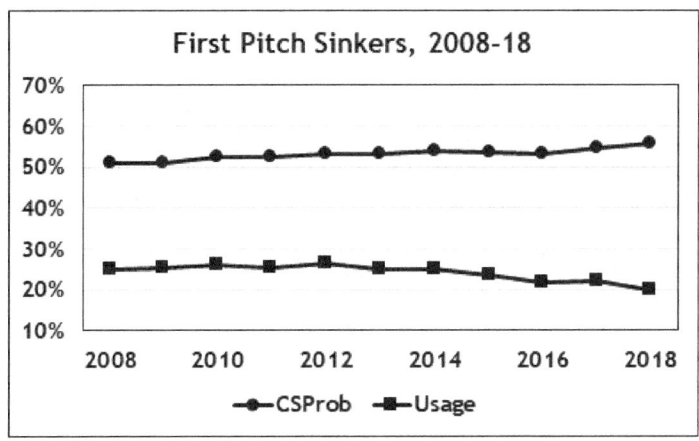

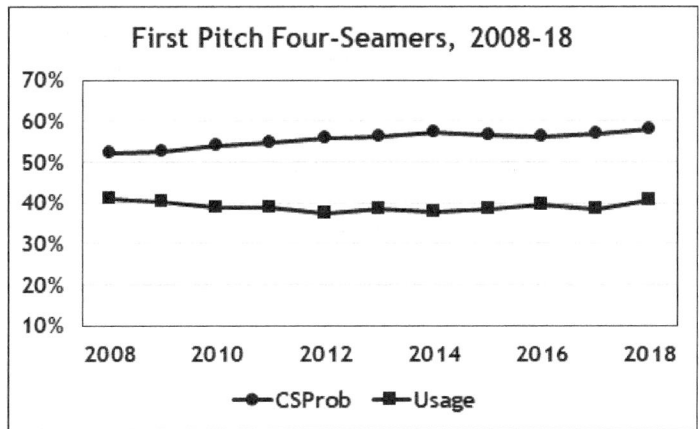

The sinker is losing its place in baseball, but the rate at which pitchers have thrown it on the first pitch hasn't dropped any faster than its usage rate in other counts. Pitchers have actually gone to their four-seamer *more* often to open counts, in the last few years, after a dip in the 2012-2015 period. What's really changed, though, and what shows up in both charts above, is that pitchers are catching more of the zone with first-pitch fastballs than they were a decade ago, or a half-decade ago. They're attacking right away, even with the pitch they know batters are expecting. The message is pretty clear: batters are being too passive.

Sliders, curves, and changeups each have more of the zone when thrown on the first pitch than they did several years ago, too, though the effect is less pronounced. Pitchers have seen the numbers; they know batters are doing better on the first pitch itself. They still feel safe throwing more and better strikes than ever before, figuring they'll come out ahead as long as they keep getting ahead to open each battle.

The Moneyball revolution brought an increased league-wide focus on OBP, which resulted in a de facto mandate to take a more patient tack at the plate. It worked very well for a while, as batters with poor plate discipline were compelled to either adjust or be expelled from the league, and pitchers with poor control were slowly weeded out.

However, concurrent with that revolution, and spurred by it in some ways, was the evolution of the pitching paradigm that now dominates the game. As batters ratcheted up their focus on inflating pitch counts and working walks, pitchers honed theirs on throwing strikes and missing bats. The league's understanding of what makes a good pitcher improved at least as much, from the mid-1990s through the mid-2000s, as its understanding of what makes a good hitter. As amphetamines and other performance-enhancing drugs were phased mostly out of the game, and as PITCHf/x broke onto the scene, individuals and teams learned how to exploit the evolved approaches of even the smartest hitters.

The ability to avoid making outs is still the most valuable one in baseball, but the magnitude of its eclipse of slugging is smaller than ever. To a greater extent than power, on-base skills derive their value from chaining—from the on-base skill levels of the players on either side of a given individual. Eleven years ago, when the housing crisis hit, people learned the hard way that the value of their homes depended a good deal on the values of their neighbors' homes. The same wasn't true, though, of their cars. So it is now, with OBP and SLG.

The global OBP in 2018 was .318. The only seasons since the Dead Ball Era in which the league got on base at a worse clip were 2013-2015, 1988, 1971-1972, and 1963-1968. This is all happening despite the aforementioned evolution of the science of hitting. It's happening despite a shift in approach and focus, one that would steer OBP ever higher, if only it were working.

Instead, it's sitting at a low ebb, and while it does so, even guys who get on base often are a little less helpful than they were 10 years ago—or 20, or 40, or 60, or 70, or 80, or 90. They're less helpful, that is, because unless there happen to be three or four other guys in the lineup who get on just as regularly, their contribution is merely to forestall the inevitable. Runs happen, increasingly, when a sudden bang happens, and that means attacking early in the count—because pitchers are sure as hell doing that.

In a league making contact on barely 75 percent of its swings, and a league in which an increasing number of pitchers can throw multiple off-speed pitches for strikes in any count, the only way to consistently generate offense is going to be aggressive. This isn't necessarily true for individuals, like Mookie Betts and Jose Ramirez, who make a lot of contact and have excellent plate discipline, and whose power comes from such natural quickness in a short stroke. Most players have to make tradeoffs, though, whether it be lowering their contact rate or raising their chase rate, in order to consistently make the quality of contact necessary to survive in today's game.

Highest %	Lowest %
Javier Baez – 48.3	Joe Mauer – 4.6
Freddie Freeman – 47.1	Mookie Betts – 9.7
Ozzie Albies – 46.3	Brett Gardner – 10.7
Jose Altuve – 44.2	Jose Ramirez – 12.0
Nick Castellanos – 44.1	Jason Kipnis – 13.8
Joey Gallo – 42.3	Jesus Aguilar – 14.5
Corey Dickerson – 40.9	Xander Bogaerts – 15.8
Salvador Perez – 40.8	Brian Dozier – 16.3
Eddie Rosario – 40.7	Mike Trout – 17.6
Nick Ahmed – 40.4	Yasmani Grandal – 17.6

Top 10 and Bottom 10 Hitters, First-Pitch Swing Rate (2018)

The question isn't which of these lists one prefers, but what they each convey, qualitatively, about the cat-and-mouse game of early-count hitting. Those top five on the left, especially, drive home the fact that for most players, getting aggressive early in the count is now key to keeping strikeout rate down and hitting for power.

For now, the message is: pitchers are coming right after batters with the nastiest stuff they've ever had. Batters had better stop giving away strike one and force hurlers to adjust, or the global OBP crisis is only going to get worse.

—*Matthew Trueblood is an author of Baseball Prospectus.*

A Hymn for the Index Stat

Patrick Dubuque

We survived without computers. I know this, because I remember the day when my dad hooked up his brand-new Atari 400 computer to the back of our 12-inch Magnavox television, and the perfect blue of the memo pad lit up for the first time. I was born just on the edge of that transitional generation, of learning cursive and balancing checkbooks and just doing math all the time, constant manual arithmetic.

It still amazes me. We learned how to sail ships without computers. We learned how to do calculus. We built towers that didn't fall down, most of the time. We engineered catapults to knock them down anyway. We built a robust system of philosophy called "utilitarianism," founded on the principle that the good of an action is evaluated by summing the effects of that action, which is the kind of formula that would make the world's mainframes crash. The whole foundation of statistics as a field is "here's math you could easily do but would die of old age first."

The fact of the matter is that there is too much math in the world to do. There are too many things changing, and too many things too small to notice, for us to handle. At some point, they become too much for the computers to handle as well, which is why we have chaos theory and undetectable earthquakes, but it's not an even fight. At some point, we fall back on intuition, and given how under-equipped we are, we're forced to bestow that intuition with some sort of supernatural superiority, the "gut feeling," that we can't prove because we can only intuit that our intuition is better.

We're all lousy at intuition, and wonderful at lying to ourselves about it. The honest truth is that computers are far better at intuition than we are, because in order to know what feels "off" you have to know what's "on." In order to do that you have to constantly reassess the average of everything, then re-rank your own experience against it.

Test your own, by comparing these three anonymous lines:

Player	G	HR	AVG	OBP	SLG
Player A	156	38	.259	.342	.535
Player B	154	38	.280	.348	.527
Player C	158	38	.266	.343	.509

These all seem like pretty similar players, right? The second one a touch more batted-ball dependent, the third a little less strong, but all pretty good hitters. And you'd be right, about the latter. Not the former.

Here's the breakdown:

- Player A: 1991 Howard Johnson, 141 DRC+
- Player B: 1996 Dean Palmer, 121 DRC+
- Player C: 2018 Giancarlo Stanton, 114 DRC+

Baseball is fortunate to have escaped the seismic shifts of so many other sports, where the talents and performances of other eras are nearly unrecognizable. (And not just other sports: try to explain the greatness of the movie Duck Soup without adjusting for era.) But they're still there, and they're nearly impossible to account for manually, without having to resort to sweeping generalizations like "steroid era" or juiced-ball era" to throw out entire swathes of production.

This is all to say that we should celebrate the index stat, that simple 100-based scale with such a humble aim: just to give context. It's hard to imagine how we lived without them for so long. Sabermetricians have always tried to make their stats look like other stats: True Average mapped to batting average, FIP molded to look like and compare to ERA. It's easy to understand the motivation—these statistics carry an emotional value in them that is hard to resist, as with the .300 hitter and the 2.00 ERA—but even they fall prey to the same loss of scale as their unadjusted counterparts. If a .300 average means different things in different years, does that hold true for a .300 True Average?

Instead, 100 doesn't say anything, except above average or below. And it does it instantly, for every season in every run environment for any statistic we want it to. We should have more index stats: K%+, so we can stop comparing Mike Clevinger's career 9.46 K/9 to Nolan Ryan's 9.55. HBP%+, so we can note that Ron Hunt was getting plunked when nobody else was getting plunked, as opposed to that imitator Brandon Guyer. Some might note how stale these references are and accuse league-adjustment as a backward-looking drive, and this is true. But we're always looking backward, always comparing the new with the expectations already set. The index stat just forces us to be honest.

There's always resistance to a new statistic, especially one so outwardly simple and so internally complex. We tend to stick with what we know, even in the case of formulas that are supposed to tell us what we know. But if your resistance is that it seems too complicated, too counterintuitive, too "black boxy," I encourage you to consider why you feel that way. Because the real world is infinitely more complicated than baseball, where all the pitches go in one basic direction and the baserunners are only allowed to travel in four directions. Baseball statistics based on mixed methodology are almost impossibly intricate. So are skyscrapers and automobiles. That's why we have computers—to take the guesswork out of them.

—Patrick Dubuque is an author of Baseball Prospectus.

Index of Names

Adon, Melvin 105
Anderson, Shaun 95, 108
Andreoli, John 104
Avelino, Abiatal 84
Bart, Joey 85, 107
Beede, Tyler 96, 111
Belt, Brandon 20
Blach, Ty 50
Black, Ray 52
Bond, Aaron 104
Bumgarner, Madison 54
Callahan, Jamie 105
Canario, Alexander 86, 109
Corry, Seth 97
Crawford, Brandon 22
Cueto, Johnny 56
De Paula, Juan 105
Doval, Camilo 98
Duggar, Steven 24
Dyson, Sam 58
Fabian, Sandro 87
Garcia, Aramis 26, 112
Gerber, Mike 88
Gonzalez, Jacob 89, 114
Gonzalez, Merandy 60
Gott, Trevor 105
Hanson, Alen 28
Herb, Tyler 105
Hjelle, Sean 99, 110
Holland, Derek 62
Howard, Ryan 90

Johnson, Chase 105
Jones, Ryder 104
Law, Derek 105
Longoria, Evan 30
Lopez, Jose 105
Marshall, Mac 113
Maybin, Cameron 32
Melancon, Mark 64
Miller, Jalen 91, 113
Moronta, Reyes 66
Okert, Steven 105
Panik, Joe 34
Parra, Gerardo 36
Phillips, Aaron 100
Pomeranz, Drew 68
Posey, Buster 38
Quinn, Heath 92, 110
Ramos, Heliot 93, 108
Rivera, Rene 104
Rodriguez, Dereck 70
Rogers, Tyler 105
Ruotolo, Patrick 105
Samardzija, Jeff 72
Sandoval, Pablo 40
Santos, Gregory 101
Shaw, Chris 94, 112
Slater, Austin 42
Smith, Will 74
Solarte, Yangervis 44
Stassi, Brock 104
Stratton, Chris 76

San Francisco Giants 2019

Suarez, Andrew	78	Watson, Tony	82
Toribio, Luis	104	Webb, Logan	102, 109
Valera, Breyvic	46	Williams, Garrett	103
Venditte, Pat	105	Williamson, Mac	48
Vincent, Nick	80	Wong, Jake	105, 113

Ballpark diagrams for Baseball Prospectus are created by THIRTY81Project, a design concept offering original ballpark artwork, including the new 'Ballparks of 2019' 11 x 17 color print.

Visit **www.thirty81project.com** for full details.

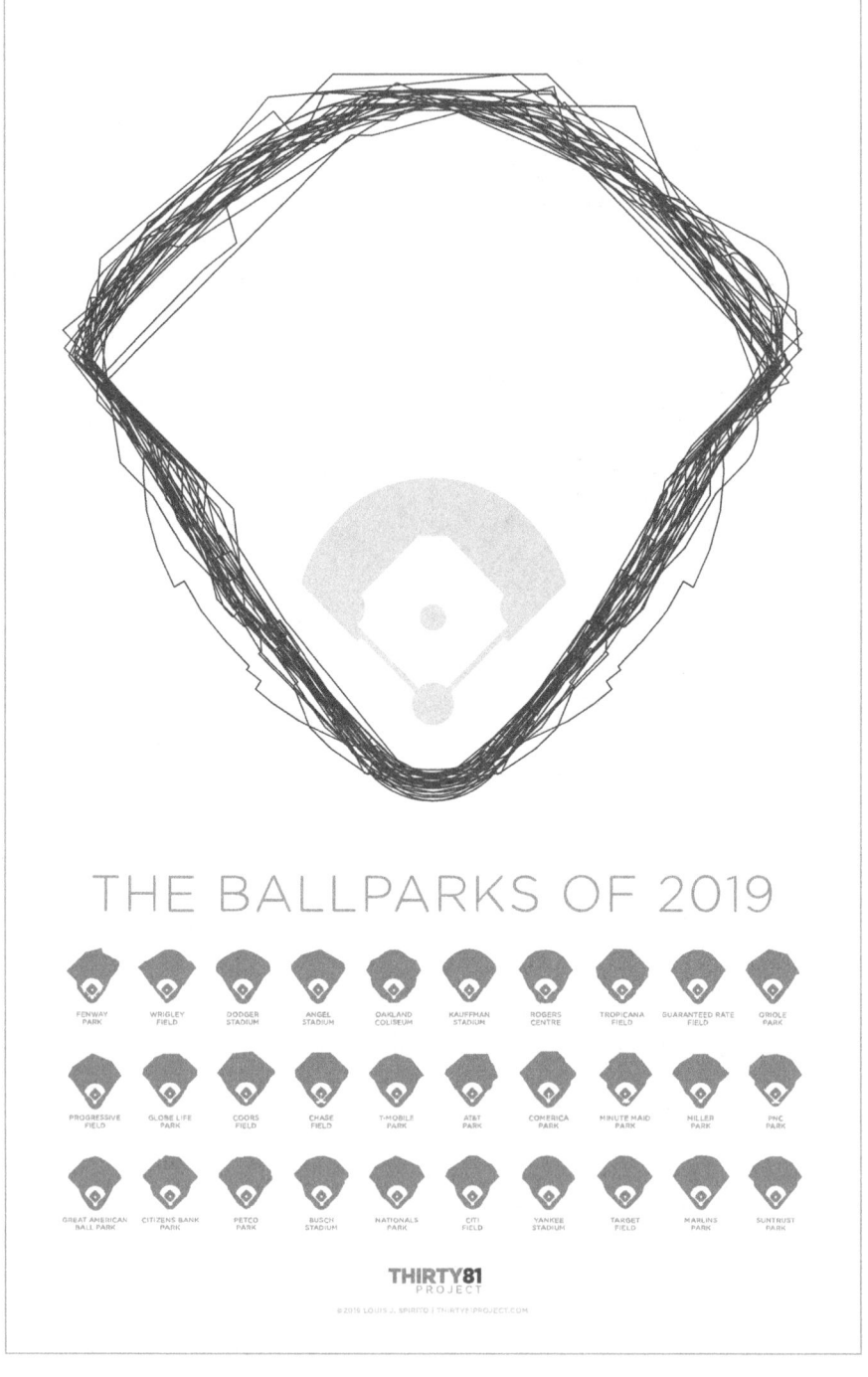